THE HIGH STRANGENESS OF BRADSHAW RANCH

RONALD C. MEYER
MARK REEDER
ALAN MEGARGLE

OTHER BOOKS BY RONALD C. MEYER
AND MARK REEDER

Tricksters and Angels

Aliens 2035: The End Of Technology

The Bigfoot Alien Connection Revisited

CONTENTS

PREFACE

In September 2022, I had just concluded speaking at the Phenomenon Conference in Vernal, Utah, with my co-producer, Alan Megargle, when it occurred to me that we needed to find a paranormal hotspot to conclude the follow-up film to our highly successful movie: *The Bigfoot Alien Connection Revealed*. That movie used the Owl Moon Lab, located south of Eugene, Oregon, to show the feasibility of multiple paranormal phenomena occurring in a specific geographical area over a long time.

Alan and I first made plans to investigate a Bigfoot and UFO site in Western Pennsylvania. However, the opportunity fell through when severe winter weather set in. We needed to find another paranormal hotspot. The very next day, I checked my newsfeed. The first item was a link describing Sedona, Arizona, as one of the world's great spiritual centers.

From this moment on, the dominoes of synchronicity fell in an unerring line directly toward a paranormal hotspot that shared many of the high strangeness qualities of Skinwalker Ranch but which was relatively unknown to the general public at the time.

My first step was to contact psychics in the Sedona area. One of them directed me to a sensitive and Bigfoot researcher from

Colorado, now living in Florida. CJ Mulkerrin had visited Bradshaw Ranch just outside of Sedona, where she had had a strange experience. She stood beside the enigmatic windmill on the property whose blades were frozen. When the blades suddenly started turning, the unusual event startled her, so she left.

CJ gave me the name of a woman in Sedona who could tell the team about the paranormal phenomena that regularly occurred at Bradshaw Ranch. Melinda Leslie is a well-known paranormal investigator who leads night viewing tours of UFOs and UAP's outside of Sedona.

I called Leslie, and she substantiated how unusual Bradshaw Ranch was and suggested that I contact Tom Dongle. Tom and the ranch's owner, Linda Bradshaw, had conducted the original paranormal research in the 90s.

Tom was very amenable and described some of the unusual things on the property during his days at the ranch. Though unable to do field research, Tom explained he was mentoring a young man, Juergen Hess, to continue his research projects on the ranch.

So, I called Juergen and had a very exciting conversation about the ranch and all the strange things happening on the property—strange things that included unusual footprints, Bigfoot sightings, UAPs, and orbs. I asked Juergen if he would be willing to be our guide if the team were to come out and film on the property. Having made a film on the ranch, Juergen was very excited about possibly working with a professional film crew. Interestingly, at the time we concluded filming at Bradshaw Ranch, Hess confided to the team that the experience had changed him from a Bigfoot researcher to a paranormal researcher.

The dominoes had fallen into place through a sequence of synchronicities, and it seemed as if my team was destined to investigate Bradshaw Ranch as a paranormal hotspot. But what underscored the urgency of the investigation was an unexplained moment of high strangeness during my phone call with Juergen. At one point during the conversation, something took control of my phone and manipulated it to show myself on the screen for about a minute. When it happened, I told Juergen, "Something has just turned my phone into a video selfie." Juergen immediately replied, "Mine too." I took this strange event as an indication that something was aware of what the team was planning to do and was, in fact, encouraging us to do the investigation.

Within two weeks, I was fortunate enough to pull together on short notice a professional film crew and a dedicated research team to investigate the reported high strangeness of Bradshaw Ranch.

Personally, my long film career began in public television. Later, I founded my own film distribution company during the rise of cable television. I produced and directed four feature films with well-known Hollywood actors during that time. After selling the distribution company to Discover Communication, I focused on creating an educational series.

My initial foray into the paranormal was launched in 2016 when Mill Creek Entertainment asked me to produce a documentary series on Bigfoot. The experience of producing the series suggested that while people had genuine contact events with an unusual creature called Bigfoot, evidence suggested that these creatures might be paraphysical or alien in nature. This revelation sparked a drive to understand paranormal phenomena, and I began to produce paranormal series and documentary features.

I formed a film production partnership with my son-in-law, Alan Megargle. Alan is a long-time sensitive and Bigfoot researcher. Together, we have produced and directed award-winning paranormal series and documentary features.

We then called upon longtime Hollywood professional Joel Meyer-England to join the team as the main camera operator. Finally, Juergen Hess was our guide and would become our eyes on Bradshaw Ranch during our absence.

Four months after the initial investigation had concluded, the team conducted a second, more intensive group of experiments on the ranch. In addition to the original team, five female psychics, including CJ Mulkerrin, were brought onto the property to see what they might sense was occurring on Bradshaw Ranch. Also, published scientist and electrical engineer Benjamin Lonetree brought his handcrafted magnetometer and computer processing hardware to capture electronically what might show up during our final night's experiment. During this experiment, we interacted with and filmed an alien intelligence for over twenty minutes.

The following experts were used in the documentary to help understand and explain the high strangeness of Bradshaw Ranch.

Dr. Simeon Hein is the director of the Institute for Resonance in Boulder, Colorado. The Institute is devoted to studying subtle-energy sciences, including remote viewing and related subjects. His latest research focuses on new physics possibilities, including interdimensional manifestations, associated plasma balls, and the potentials of the fifth state of matter that occurs when atoms are so densely packed that they behave in novel ways.

John B. Alexander, Ph.D., is a retired United States Army colonel. His assignments have included Commander, Army Special Forces Teams; US Army Thailand and Vietnam; and Director of the Advanced Concepts US Army Lab. In 1985, Alexander founded the Advanced Theoretical Physics Project, an informal cadre of 'government officials'—including "people from the Army, Navy, and Air Force, plus several from the defense aerospace industries and some members from the Intelligence Community"—who "took it upon themselves to find out whether there was a secret federal UFO project." Alexander characterizes his career as having "evolved from hard-core mercenary to thanatologist." Alexander figures prominently in journalist Jon Ronson's book *The Men Who Stare At Goats*, which was later made into a Hollywood film starring George Clooney. Alexander was one of the lead scientists who investigated Skinwalker Ranch when aerospace pioneer Robert Bigelow owned it.

Tom Dongo is a long-time resident of Sedona. During this time, he has camped on and hiked over thousands of miles of the Sedona/Flagstaff/Prescott mountains, mesas, deserts, and canyons. He is a recognized world authority on UFOs and paranormal occurrences. Tom Dongo's most popular book is *Merging Dimensions: The Incredible Saga of the Bradshaw Ranch*. He said what happened to him on Bradshaw Ranch produced his superhuman capability of x-ray body vision, verified by Stanford Research Lab.

Melinda Leslie is a researcher, investigator, and lecturer in the field of Ufology. For over twenty years, she has been public with her own abduction experiences, researched covert-ops and military involvement in abductions (also known as MILABs), and has interviewed over eighty abductees. In addition to her abduction work, Melinda has been a paranormal researcher for over twenty-five years, including Bradshaw Ranch, and is a founding member of the Orange County Paranormal Researchers.

The investigative research team eventually put together a remarkable documentary feature: *The Mysteries Of Bradshaw Branch: Aliens, Portals and the Paranormal.* However, when it was done, there was much more to the Bradshaw Ranch investigation than could be explored in a 90-minute feature.

I once more enlisted the aid of Mark Reeder, my co-author on our first book—*The Bigfoot Alien Connection Revisited*—to help me expand the content of the documentary into a book that could explore the profound connection of Bradshaw Ranch's high strangeness and a rapidly developing understanding of a new kind of physics. If it is true that Bradshaw is a place of interdimensional portals, then the main hypothesis is that different universes are merging with different physical constants. If true, this possibly could answer the most profound question humans pose about themselves: Are we alone in the universe?

Ron Meyer, November 18th 2023

1

SEDONA, ARIZONA, AND BRADSHAW RANCH: HISTORY AND GEOLOGICAL SETTING

From the moment we first stepped foot in Sedona, Arizona, the area's breathtaking beauty grabbed hold of us and wouldn't let go. In the heart of the Coconino National Forest, Sedona is known for its deep red rock mesas and spectacular pinnacles that thrust into a deep blue sky like church spires. The steep-sided canyons and forested valleys are home to a plenitude of animal life. At night, Sedona is a dark sky city, and the brilliance of the Milky Way galaxy shines its benevolence like a benediction upon all who gaze in wonder at the star-filled night sky.

In the 21st century, Sedona has become more than a touristy oasis for those seeking to commune with the beauty of northern Arizona's high desert and experience awakenings. Today, visitors can book tours of Sedona's vortexes and experience the city as one of the Desert Southwest's premier spiritual centers. Once darkness emerges, using military-grade night vision goggles, people join sky watch tours and spot dozens of UAPs and UFOs crisscrossing the night sky.

On the other hand, the paranormal refers to phenomena beyond the scope of current consensus scientific explanation and understanding. This includes psychic abilities like ESP as well as documented events such as UFO, ghost, and Bigfoot sightings. While some people may believe paranormal phenomena are spiritual, there is no conclusive evidence to support this claim.

Figure 1: Aerial View of Sedona Area, Including Red Rock Mesas, High Desert, and Scrubland

Figure 2: Aerial View of a Vortex Mesa

Our team did not go to Arizona to investigate Sedona's spiritual wonders. We were in the high desert to examine the many documented paranormal events at Bradshaw Ranch.

Upon arriving in the Sedona area, our team did an extensive on-camera interview with Tom Dongo in Cottonwood, Arizona. He suggested we join paranormal investigator Melinda Leslie on her night sky-watching tour. It's hard to explain just how magnificent the night sky appears through these high-resolution goggles.

Figure 3: Sedona Night Sky Through Night Vision Goggles Showing UAP and Laser Beam

What we saw was mind-blowing. Within an hour, we spotted at least forty objects crisscrossing the sky. A couple were in the formation of twos and fours. But the most amazing aspect was that Leslie would take her green light laser and flash it on the brightest orange UAPs, and they would respond by flashing back at her. With some fast-thinking adjustments to our cameras, we were able to record this phenomenon.

Later, back in our hotel room, a little research revealed that the most satellites and space junk one could expect to see within an hour would not exceed two dozen objects. Overall, the experience, though hard to explain, augured a good beginning to our investigation.

Sedona did not start off as a new-age spiritual Mecca. Thousands of years ago, the area's unusual properties first attracted the Southwest Desert's Native Americans, who depicted shamans, important animals, and occasional paranormal phenomena in petroglyphs and pictographs on the surrounding red rock cliffs.

White settlers appeared in the late 19th century, setting up farms and ranches. Later, beginning in the 1920s, Sedona's colorful landscape played host to Hollywood productions for fifty years, including the classic westerns: *3:10 to Yuma* and *Angel and the Badman*. Then, in the 1950s, Sedona began development as a tourist destination, vacation retreat, and retirement city.

It wasn't until the 21st century that the draw to the area became much more than the natural beauty of the high desert and scrubland. Sedona is now a significant destination for people hoping to have a spiritual experience as a result of its vortexes. In fact, many people have reported that the Sedona vortexes are particularly powerful and can enhance meditation, self-discovery, and spiritual growth. The vortexes are associated with four specific sites in the Sedona area: Cathedral Rock, Bell Rock, Airport Mesa, and Boynton Canyon.

Figure 4: Benjamin Lonetree at Bradshaw Ranch

Benjamin Lonetree spent years looking into the nature of the vortexes, locating and measuring them with his specially designed and built magnetometer. He confirmed that the vortexes were powerful magnetic fields that fluctuated in space and time. That is, they were not permanent and moved around on the red rock mesas.

Lonetree developed a probable explanation for Sedona as a

spiritual center. An electrical engineer by training, he explained to us that the area's surface red rocks are heavy with iron. Massive quartzite deposits lie below the iron strata. He theorizes that the positive ion spikes and magnetic fluctuations radiating from the strata light up like a beacon—a kind of radio transmitter or receiver for alien contact. In fact, it has been argued by several leading scientists this combination of ions and magnetism could be used to open portals to other dimensions, including at nearby Bradshaw Ranch.

Figure 5a: Bob Bradshaw

Figure 5b: John Bradshaw

Just a short distance away as the crow flies, Bradshaw Ranch shares Sedona's underlying geological formations of iron and quartz. The ranch also shares a similar history. Sitting beneath soaring red rock mesas, Bradshaw Ranch had a prosaic start, homesteaded in the early 20th century by pioneers looking to fulfill the American dream and make a living in Arizona's high desert. The family built a simple adobe homestead.

In 1960, Bob Bradshaw bought the property, who turned the sprawling 180-acre ranch into a movie set. When he moved in, all that remained of the original ranch, which had been abandoned in 1942, was the old adobe homestead, which still stands today and is believed to be the oldest pioneer structure still standing in the Sedona area.

Over the years, the Bradshaw Ranch has been a location for Hollywood productions. For the 1967 film *Stay Away Joe* starring Elvis Presley, an old town known as Bitter Creek was built. The set was later used for five movies, two television series, and numerous commercials.

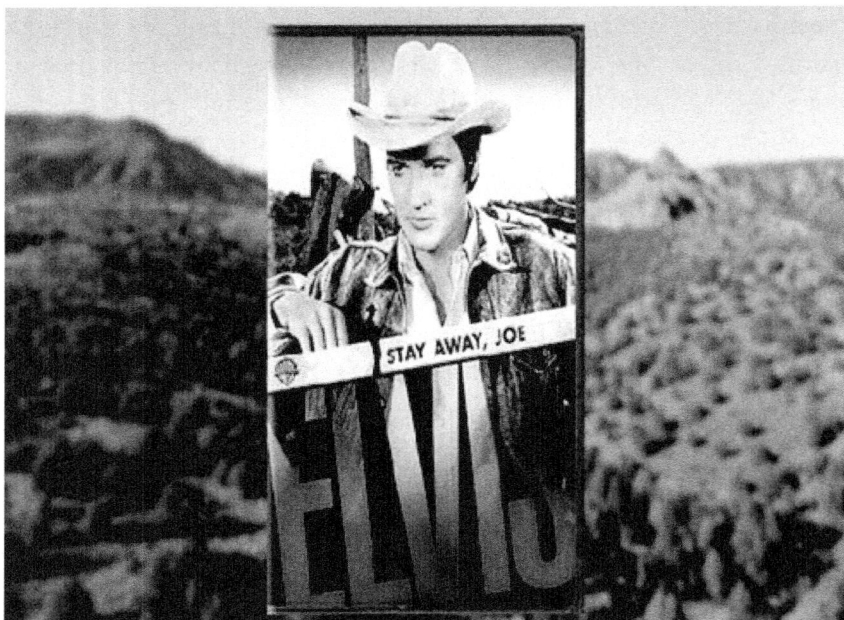

Figure 6: Elvis Presley Movie Poster 'Stay Away Joe'

Together, Bob and his wife ran the ranch's thriving commercial enterprise. But the Bradshaw Ranch had an unexpected and unusual quality. Over the years, both reported seeing strange balls of light as well as colorful orbs hovering over the landscape. Their observances led to the investigations of the ranch's high strangeness by Bob's son, John, and his wife, Linda.

Eventually, John took over the management of the Bradshaw Ranch, using it as a tourist destination for horseback rides and jeep tours. By the mid-90s, only Linda Bradshaw remained living on the property. That's when she began her paranormal investigations with Tom Dongo. Together, the two friends wrote a book titled *Merging Dimensions: The Opening Portals of Sedona*, describing the many paranormal phenomena they encountered on the ranch.

Linda later wrote a follow-up work, *Dimensional Journey: Encoun-*

ters and Teachings, in which she wrote that her time on the ranch 'pro-pelled her onto a journey of immense spiritual growth' that expanded her psychic abilities.

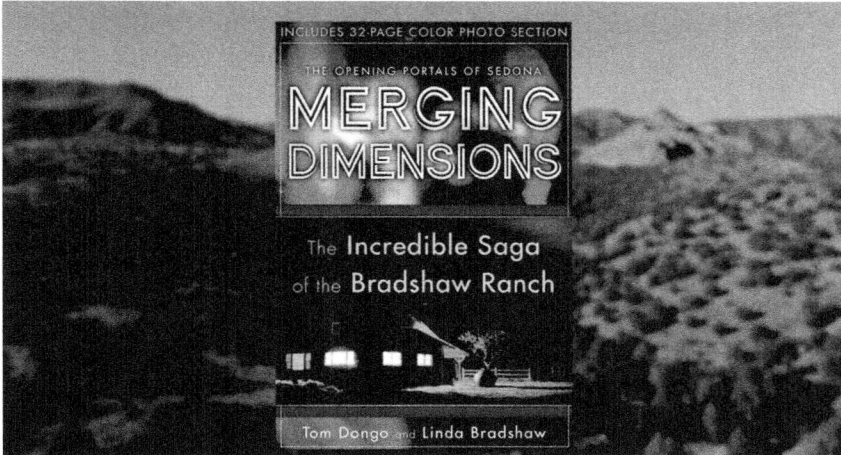

Figure 7: Tom Dongo and Linda Bradshaw's Book 'Merging Dimension's: The Opening Portals of Sedona'

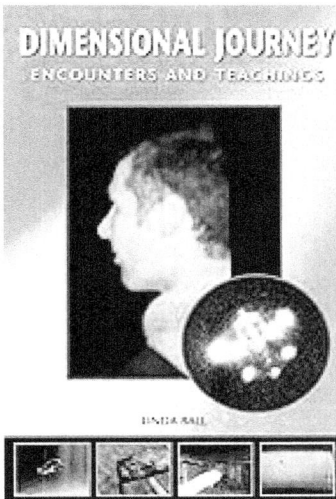

Figure 8: Linda Ball's, aka Linda Bradshaw, book 'Dimensional Journey: Encounters and Teachings'

At the dawn of the new millennium, Bradshaw Ranch became embroiled in even deeper mysteries. As best we can tell in April of 2003, the family sold the property to the U.S. government for $3.5 million. The ranch eventually became part of the Federal Forest Service. Funded by the U.S. DOE Biosciences Energy Center and coordinated by the Plant Molecular Biology Group at Oak Ridge National Laboratory in Oak Ridge, Tennessee, twenty-two acres of the Bradshaw Ranch supposedly became an experimental station for the Southwest Experimental Garden

Array (SEGA) conducting long term climate change research. A barbed wire fence was erected around that portion of the ranch, along with a locked gate, preventing entrance by anyone not associated with the SEGA project.

Soon, conspiracy theories emerged about what was really going on between the government and the ranch. Area residents reported numerous military vehicles as well as armed guards patrolling the ranch's perimeter. Many locals refuse to approach the property out of fear. Similarly, the word on the street in Sedona is that the U.S. government is covering up a virtual invasion of interdimensional entities coming through a wide-open dimensional corridor.

More recently, producers from the mega-hit television series *Beyond Skinwalker Ranch* visited the property to explore the possibility of a secret government/alien underground tunnel running from the ranch to an abandoned concrete plant to the west.

As of the publication of this book, we are still unable to confirm or deny any of these conspiracies. However, one of the psychics we brought to the property told us during her visit, "There is technology here, and it is underground, but I could not locate it."

It is important to note that during the period of our investigation, which lasted nearly six months, we were unaware of any of these conspiracies. Nor were we aware of the confusing reports about how the ranch was transferred from the Bradshaw's to the U.S. Forest Service. In fact, our investigation was not influenced by any of the conspiratorial history surrounding the ranch.

When we arrived at the property, guided by Juergen Hess, the gate was unlocked. Plenty of evidence showed many people had visited the ranch buildings, including Juergen, who, over a couple of years, had conducted research on the property almost weekly. In fact, during our second visit to Bradshaw, our trail cam recorded two instances of ordinary people entering the property, going inside the ranch house, and leaving without incident.

Interestingly, the powerful Utah multi-millionaire owner of Skinwalker ranch, Brandon Fugal, traveled to Bradshaw just after our arrival and was guided by Juergen. Eventually, Brandonattempted to purchase the property. However, the U. S. government refused to sell.

We only learned about these instances and supposed conspiracies concerning Bradshaw after we were done filming. Indeed, what we had learned from the outset through Tom Dongo, Melinda Leslie, and Juergen Hess was that the ranch was an incredibly active paranormal hotspot. And we were not to be disappointed.

2

BRADSHAW RANCH LAYOUT

O riginally, our Bradshaw Ranch investigation and filming was designed to be a ten-to-fifteen-minute conclusion to our second feature film *The Bigfoot Alien Superhuman Connection Revealed*. The plan was to spend one day and one night filming with our guide Juergen Hess, hoping some paranormal events would occur.

Upon arriving on the ranch property, Juergen was most excited about showing us some unusual tracks he had located in a dry creek bed running along the east edge of the property.

Figure 9: Bigfoot Track next to Juergen Hess's Boot Shadow at Bradshaw Ranch

We were able to film some very large prints which could be attributed to Bigfoot. In addition, we saw some interesting three-toed impressions that resembled dinosaur tracks. Indeed, during our time on the ranch, we constantly ran into unusual prints and impressions, including some from very large vehicles.

Once deeper on the property, our first act was to film all the important structures as well as the ranch's layout. Immediately upon approaching the buildings, the team realized the ranch no longer had electricity or running water, and it was obvious to everyone no one had lived there for two decades. Having produced programs related to ghost towns of the West, Ron and Alan noted the property emanated the same sense of strangeness—spooky but not scary—as old mining towns once teeming with life and were now abandoned.

Figure 10: Aerial View of Bradshaw Ranch Showing the Adobe Homestead (left) Ranch House (right), and Windmill (center)

Entering from the east end of the ranch, three prominent structures form a triangle. The old adobe homestead sets the first point. To the left and slightly ahead, the ranch house sets the second point. And directly to the north, a rusted-out windmill rises above everything, sealing the triangle's final point.

It is interesting to note that not only is the triangle one of nature's strongest and most dominant geometric shapes, but the triangle or groups of triangles are prevalent in the occult and spiritual practices because of the claim that vortexes create them. On our second visit to Bradshaw, we captured an enigmatic triangle shape on the trail cam. The triangle was translucent and positioned perfectly over an area we later referred to as the space of high strangeness. The phenomenon was later described by a Mutual UFO Network video forensic expert, Seth Feinstein, to be an interdimensional portal.[1]

Figure 11: Aerial View of Bradshaw Ranch's Corrals and Outbuildings

Proceeding west along the valley, numerous structures, including smaller buildings in various states of collapse, point out that Bradshaw was once a working ranch.

The adobe structure is quite small, with two main rooms. As in most abandoned buildings, relics from the past are scattered helter-skelter across the floors. Some of the glass windowpanes are broken, but others remain intact. And as one might expect, there is ample graffiti relating to aliens and the *X Files* meme. Interestingly, there were some modern light fixtures in the ceiling.

The ranch house is quite a different story. It's very large with many rooms, including a large kitchen, several bedrooms, and bathrooms. Just beyond the front door is a large open space with an elevated platform in the center, and to one side are the remains of what must have been a bar. Later during our stay, the team experienced the most astonishing paranormal events in this room.

Scattered throughout the other rooms are abandoned furniture, including beds that one could sleep on today. This building was once a very lively place, acting as a movie set and a restaurant. Of course, the ranch house had its own set of unnerving wall graffiti similar to what was found in the adobe homestead.

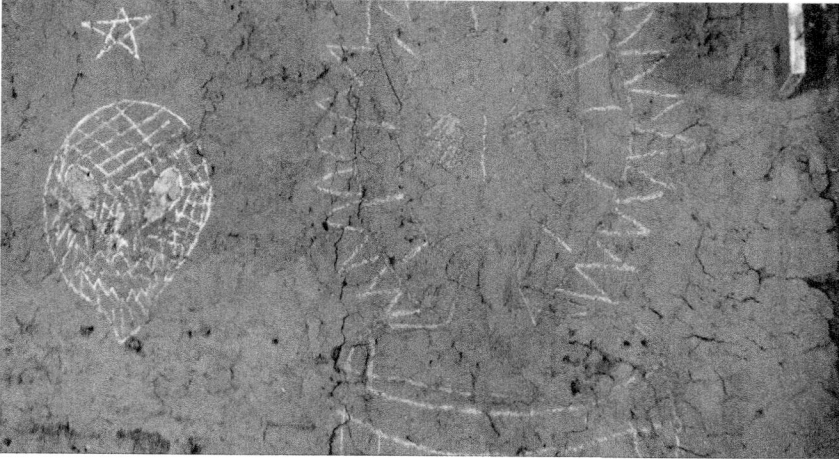

Figure 12: Graffiti on Adobe Homestead's Walls

We took the time to check for any unusual magnetic readings and electromagnetic readings in both buildings. We were disappointed when they turned out to be normal.

That left the windmill to explore and film. During his interview, Tom Dongo told the story of a Japanese film crew member who wandered up to the windmill and disappeared for a few hours. "A typical time slip," he explained. Tom told us that he would never go up to the windmill. In addition, the windmill was the spot where CJ had her unusual experience with the blades turning unexpectedly. Consequently, the team approached the third point of the triangle with a bit of trepidation.

Windmills, often called wind pumps or wind-powered water pumps, are commonly employed in rural areas to harness wind energy for various purposes, such as irrigation and supplying water to nearby buildings. Next to the Bradshaw Ranch windmill, a large tank had been used to store water drawn from an aquifer deep underground. In the back of the windmill, a wooden structure sheltered the well shaft.

Figure 13: Bradshaw Ranch Windmill and Water Tank

We decided to do our first experiment in the well enclosure and began filming. Once again, we decided to take base readings for magnetic fluctuations and any elevated electromagnetic radiation in the microwave and radio frequency range. We also set up the team's Geiger counter to see if there were any high radiation levels. Again, all was normal.

We knew from the Skinwalker Ranch series that the scientific investigation team had used a lot of technology to, as they said, 'poke the bear' and 'hope for some sort of anomalous or measurable result would show up'. In almost all cases, their high-tech equipment had been rendered inoperable by unexplainable forces. We wondered what would happen when we introduced some low-tech ghost-hunting equipment. So we broke out the REM Pod and the Spirit Box.

A REM Pod is a compact battery-powered device originally designed as a piece of paranormal ghost-hunting equipment. The

REM Pod puts out a weak radio frequency signal, and anything entering its field triggers light and temperature sensors.

The Spirit Box, also known as an Electro Voice Phenomenon Detector (EVP) is a battery-powered radio receiver employed by many ghost investigators. The device rapidly scans all available AM/FM signals in the hopes that an alien or ghostly entity can choose words in order to communicate.

Although Juergen led ghost tours and was familiar with this type of equipment, he had never heard of anyone using these devices on Bradshaw and was curious to find out what would happen when he tried to communicate by asking all the usual ghost-hunting questions. Our efforts resulted in no activity until Juergen asked, "Are there any beings here that can see us?"

The REM Pod responded with its highest level, indicating a 'yes.'

The team was excited by this reply and hoped it portended some major paranormal activity when we returned to the ranch that evening. As Juergen had told us when we first arrived, "The night is when Bradshaw really lights up."[2]

Moving on with our overview filming of the ranch, we were quickly reminded of the conspiratorial stories mentioned in the previous chapter. We found a fully modern weather station a short distance from the gated entrance, now abandoned and beginning to fall apart. The station confirmed the ranch might have been a place for climate research.

However, the most unusual occurrence lending itself to the possibility of a conspiracy was a collection of highly sophisticated and expensive ground movement sensing devices. The abandoned equipment was connected by wires running through modern conduit, eventually terminating at an information processing and controlling device powered by solar panels. Interestingly, if not peculiarly, this equipment was the same equipment that has been proposed for use in the next season of the Skinwalker Ranch television series.

According to Juergen, the equipment arrived four years before our investigation and had been abandoned for approximately two years. Nearby, an abandoned trail camera had recorded for one minute twice a day at the same time for over two years until the battery died. It is clear that bringing in and setting up this equipment had been a large-scale operation. Its intended use is no small mystery and only adds to the aura of conspiracy surrounding the once thriving and now deserted ranch.

Figure 14: Alan Megargle with Hi-Tech Sensor Equipment Left Behind at Bradshaw Ranch

The day had been long, and the team was eager to head back to Sedona for dinner and some rest before we began the night phase of the investigation. But before leaving, we decided to launch a drone and capture aerials of the ranch and the surrounding area. The peaceful high desert under a late afternoon sun was as glorious as a Georgia O'Keefe landscape. Yet, even the drone footage captured an underlying tension that Bradshaw Ranch seemed to project into the late fall day. The team, in turn, sensed an urgency in our mission to investigate the Ranch and its paranormal activities. We could hardly wait to return when darkness set in.

---

1. See Appendix A on the importance of triangles to ancient humans and modern-day mystery schools and practices.

2. The experiment at the windmill was the first occurrence at the ranch, where Ron felt the compulsion of synchronicity. In this case, the impulse resulted not only in filming the windmill but in setting up the first experiment conducted by the team. In the moment, Ron had a clear sense that something important would happen if the team performed the experiment. Looking upon the windmill, Ron remembered that Tom Dongo had said in his interview that Linda Bradshaw and he had often felt alien entities on the ranch that could see them but which they could not see. Tom also said, "Sometimes it was like being in Grand Central Station." The experiment at the windmill yielded a very important question that we would use to trigger paranormal phenomena: 'Is there something here that can see us?'

3

THE TIME SLIP

A 'time slip' typically refers to a paranormal experience where an individual or a group of people perceives a temporary and unexplained displacement in time.[1] One of the more common forms of a time slip is associated with abduction experiences. Individuals often claim no time passed from the moment they were taken to the moment they were returned. Another form is when an individual or group participates in an activity, particularly during a paranormal investigation, and later has no memory of that participation.

Our investigation team has encountered the phenomena of 'time slips' on several occasions, including one that occurred when Alan Megargle and the team were filming an experiment just outside of Skinwalker Ranch. In Alan's case, he talked about feeling weird while standing beside the REM pod. While filming him, we thought he was acting strangely, saying incoherent things. But when reviewing the footage, we showed Alan video confirmation of what happened. These time slips are very disconcerting to people, and often, they are quite shocked when they see the video footage. Alan shook his head and declared, "I have no memory of that at all."

At the end of our first day at Bradshaw Ranch, we headed back to Sedona for some rest and dinner. We had decided to return to the property that night to continue filming and conducting experiments. Juergen suggested we arrive at midnight. For some reason, this didn't feel right to Ron. He called Tom Dongo to ask the veteran researcher what we should do. Tom emphatically advised us to arrive no later than 7 PM. Juergen agreed.

Figure 15: Alan Megargle Beside the Rem Pod at Skinwalker Ranch

The route from Sedona to Bradshaw starts by taking State Highway 179 south to a right-hand turn onto a gravel road. Driving from the highway on the gravel road to the ranch takes exactly one-half hour. We agreed to meet Juergen in a parking area at the junction of the highway and the gravel road. At 6:30, Juergen joined us in our large rental vehicle. It was dark as we headed towards the ranch. The road is straightforward as long as one doesn't deviate by taking any of the side roads that wind through the high desert scrubland. Juergen had driven the road many times and was very confident we would have no trouble reaching the ranch at 7 o'clock.

We hadn't traveled far from the highway along the gravel road, when a feeling of disorientation overcame all of us. The confusion began when we noticed that what we saw out the car's windows made no sense. Instead of desert chaparral, we looked upon buildings and lights that were totally out of place in the northern Arizona wilderness.

Much more than half an hour passed with no sign of Bradshaw ranch anywhere. At one point, we drove up a steep hill to a dead end. In the pitch dark, the severity of our situation was not lost on any of us. We could have driven off a cliff or into an arroyo, and no one would have found us for days or weeks.

With much trepidation, we all agreed we were lost. Then, almost miraculously, we found ourselves once more on the road to Bradshaw. It seemed nearly an hour had passed since we left the junction of the highway and were back on the correct road. Inexplicably, we arrived on time at 7 PM.

We couldn't account for the extra thirty minutes of time we experienced in the desert wandering the back roads. On the other hand, one could say it took no time at all for the rest of the ordinary world. Multiple perspectives aside, our vehicle's GPS had tracked our journey out of time and showed us weaving around like drunken sailors for the half hour we were *lost*. Lost is italicized because in all fairness to the team's experience and the eventual outcome of arriving at Bradshaw Ranch on time at 7:00pm, perhaps we weren't really lost at all. Perhaps our personal 'time slip' had been part of Bradshaw Ranch's high strangeness, putting us in the altered state of mind necessary to experience what was to follow that night.[2]

Moreover, the synchronicity of our 'time slip' experience was underscored in another way. Often reported in conjunction with Bradshaw are large orange, ball-shaped UAPs. In fact, our guide Juergen has captured a sequence of this phenomenon with his still camera.

Dr. Simeon Hein, director of the Institute for Resonance in Boulder, Colorado, theorizes, "This is incoherent, ordinary matter, shifting into the fifth state of matter, which is called coherent matter, where all the particles have given up their individuality to become at the same temperature and at the same frequency. When that happens, electrons can escape, and they become ball lightning or orbs. Also, during this process, there are simultaneous changes in the speed of light producing 'times slips'."

Figures 16a; 16b; and 16c: Juergen Hess's Pictures of an Orange UAP Changing Position and Shape Over Bradshaw Ranch

This phenomenon has been documented at Skinwalker ranch. This phenomenon of merging two universes with different physical constants is part of the new physics at Bradshaw ranch. We would encounter this phenomenon again on our second visit to Bradshaw.

---

1. A classic example of a time slip is the Charles Dickens novel, *A Christmas Carol*. For nonfictional accounts of time slips go to https://listverse.com/2021/01/26/ten-amazing-slips-in-time/#:~:text=3%20Versailles,a%20wood%20worked%20in%20tapestry.
2. A time slip is not be confused with time travel, time loops, or time fugues. A time slip is a loss of time due to a paranormal event. Time travel is a plot device in fantasy and science fiction, where an individual or a group travels through time deliberately, using a device called a time machine. H. G. Welles' *The Time Machine* is considered the progenitor of all time travel novels. A time loop or temporal loop is a plot device in fiction whereby characters re-experience a span of time which is repeated, sometimes more than once, as in the Bill Murray movie *Groundhog Day*. A time fugue is a dissociative state in humans that may last from hours to months and occasionally longer.

4

THE FIRST PORTAL

The plan for the team's first night investigation was to carry out typical ghost-hunting experiments in both the adobe homestead and the ranch house to see if we could interact with any entities. We started in the ranch house. Our ghost-hunting toolkit included a handheld K-2 EMF Meter for detecting magnetic fluctuations, the REM pod, and the spirit box. In addition, Alan had downloaded the GhostTube SLS (Structured Light Sensor) app on his android-based smartphone. The app allows paranormal investigators to detect invisible human shapes and movements and displays them as stick figures on the screen. This effect is achieved using complex AI algorithms to detect human poses and shapes.

With the equipment set up, we began our experiment by trying to speak with the ghost of John Bradshaw. Several minutes passed with no response. Juergen next tried to connect with Linda Bradshaw. Again, nothing. Then he asked, "Is there something here that can see us?"

Instantly, Alan felt the presence of something and was compelled to open the GhostTube SLS app. Against the room's western wall, a human figure was detected. Alan walked towards the entity with the K-2 EMF Meter in hand. The light indicators lit up as he approached.

Upon reaching the wall, Alan felt an intense column of cold. He thrust the meter into the cold and the EMF readings spiked, indicating high magnetic fluctuations.

Figure 17: Alan and Juergen Experience the Column of Cold Air Beside the Wall in the Ranch House

Alan called Juergen over, and together, they confirmed the presence of the extreme column of cold air as well as the high reading on the meter. Once more employing the SLS app, Alan saw a perfect human stick figure sitting on a nearby sink.

Paranormal literature has long speculated that when alien entities materialize or portals are opened to our world, they require immense energy. Drawing that energy from the surrounding environment causes a sudden drop in temperature that can be experienced and recorded. Had we just filmed the opening of a portal and the emergence of an otherwise invisible entity?Later, we described the event to Dr. Simeon Hein. He explained, "So on this continuum of coherent matter, that's what Lockheed Martin said their patent was on. It was for—creating cloaking, invisibility, teleportation, and directed energy weapons. There has to be a realm of life in matter beyond the ordinary type of matter, which would be in the same space as us, but it's not interacting with light and electromagnetics in the way we're used to. So it's going to be an invisible life form. The most shocking part of all this is that we are surrounded by lifeforms we cannot see. The name the intelligence agency gave to this [phenomenon] is dark mode plasma or stealth plasma."[1]

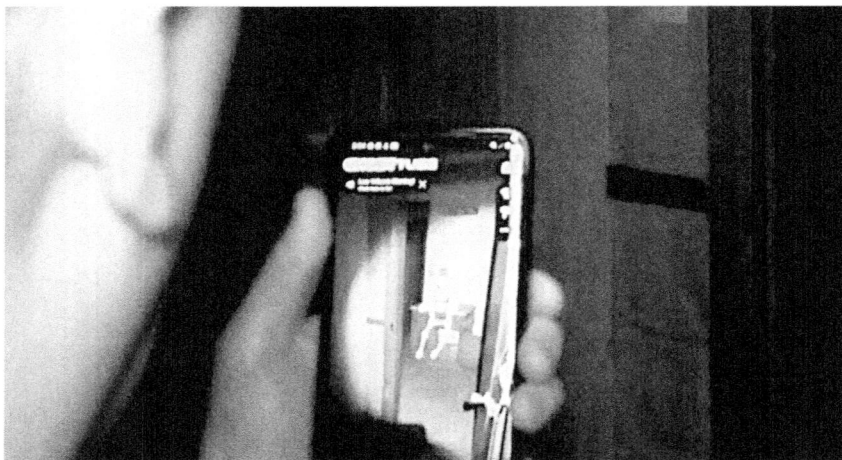

Figure 18: Android Phone SLS App Showing Stick Figure Sitting on the Vanity in the Ranch House

Data from our experiment suggest that there are indeed entities that are aware of us and maybe even guiding our actions in order to reveal themselves through technology. Nearly every human has experienced what might be called a *guiding hand*, leading us toward something of immense importance in our lives. Was something at Bradshaw pre-cognitively guiding or anticipating the team's experiments?

Retired Army Colonel John B. Alexander believes this may be the case at Bradshaw as it was during his investigations at Skinwalker Ranch. "If you're talking [about] what I was addressing about Skinwalker Ranch, I called it an 'it', and that's just because I have no way to conceptualize what an 'it' might be. I called this a precognitive sentient phenomenon. I said it was precognitive because 'it', whatever this consciousness was, 'it' knew what we would do from a scientific investigative standpoint before the event occurred. 'It' was certainly intelligent, sentient, and knew what was going on."

Interestingly, as we moved our team from the ranch house to the adobe homestead, Alan and Juergen stopped and noted the absolute dead silence surrounding us. Both were well aware of the phenomenon of dead silence and the appearance of ghosts and other paranormal phenomena. Even though it wasn't revealed to us until we viewed the footage, a bright, rapidly pulsating UAP hovered above the horizon, tracking us as we moved into the adobe homestead, where we recorded the most astounding event of the night.

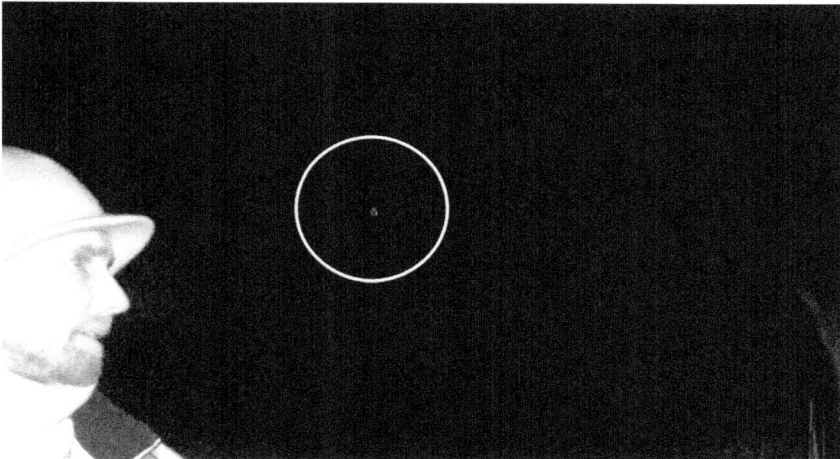

Figure 19: Juergen Hess with Pulsating UAP in the Night Sky Between the Ranch House and the Adobe Homestead

1. Since the 1950s stealth mode plasma has been very controversial and its use highly classified. Plasma stealth is a proposed process to use ionized gas (plasma) to reduce the radar cross-section (RCS) of an aircraft. Interactions between electromagnetic radiation and ionized gas have been extensively studied for many purposes, including concealing aircraft from radar as stealth technology. Various methods might plausibly be able to form a layer or cloud of plasma around a vehicle to deflect or absorb radar, from simpler electrostatic or radio frequency discharges to more complex laser discharges. It is theoretically possible to reduce RCS in this way, but it may be very difficult to do so in practice. Some Russian missiles, for example the 3M22 Zircon (SS-N-33) and Kh-47M2 Kinzhal missiles, have been reported to make use of plasma stealth. Wikipedia

5

BIGFOOT

Since 2016, Ron and Alan have produced several highly successful documentary series and feature films that explore the phenomena of Bigfoot history, sightings, and evidence, as well as examine many of the hypotheses on the nature of these cryptids. During this time, a major shift has occurred from Bigfoot being classified as some sort of unknown hominid or great hairy ape to a paraphysical being brought under the umbrella of paranormal contact experiences. Also, during this time, Ron experienced his own Bigfoot sighting, while Alan had multiple 'felt contact' experiences through telepathic communication. These experiences were extremely valuable to Alan's overall understanding of Bigfoot as an entity capable of paraphysical undertakings. However, he very much wanted to have his own personal Bigfoot sighting.

Bradshaw Ranch has had a long history with Bigfoot. As noted earlier in Chapter One, the property contains evidence of trackways that could be attributed to Bigfoot. In addition, Melinda Leslie and Tom Dongo related many accounts of Bigfoot appearances at the ranch in their interviews. So many so that Melinda Leslie told us it had a name—Big Gal. However, these notions were far from our thoughts when we entered the adobe homestead.

Once again, we set up our ghost hunting equipment on the back room floor. After several failed attempts to communicate with the dead, Alan asked, "Is there something here that can see us?"

Without warning, Alan became transfixed, staring out a window for nearly a minute and a half. Fortunately, the camera operator was filming Alan while the altered state lasted. We immediately asked Alan to tell us what he had seen when the event was over.

Figure 20: Alan Staring Transfixed at the Bigfoot Outside of the Adobe Homestead

Alan answered, "When I looked out the window, there was a black figure crouched down, and I blinked a couple of times to see if I was really seeing it, and when my eyes refocused again, it was closer. Then it moved left right, right, left right, right, left." Alan stopped and beckoned Juergen to come over in order to show him what he had seen out the window. Then he continued his story. "It was like a Bigfoot, a shadow. It stood up and then crouched down more. I was staring at it, and then it flashed ... then flashed a few more times, and it was gone."

Later, in the edit suite, when we looked at Alan's footage of seeing the Bigfoot, a small, bright white light with no apparent source of origination appeared outside of another window. However, Bradshaw Ranch had no electricity on the property, so we were puzzled about what was causing it. As we watched the footage, the light synced up with Alan as he spoke. When he mentioned that the Bigfoot-like shadow flashed, the light outside the window flashed. It acted as if it perfectly well understood what Alan was saying.

Figure 21: Image of Bright Light Hovering Outside Adobe Homestead Window While Alan Was Speaking

Figure 22: Orb Flying Toward Alan and About to Enter Him

Figure 23: Another Orb Between Alan and Juergen

In addition, the footage revealed that during our investigation, a number of what might be called orbs were moving around the room. At first, their motions appeared random. Eventually, they headed for Alan, appearing to enter him. At one point, just before he saw the Bigfoot-like shadow, Alan seemed aware of an orb as it moved toward him. We could see that he looked at something and tracked it as the possible orb moved towards him.

We used video cameras equipped with night vision during the filming in both buildings.[1] These kinds of cameras use infrared LEDs, which emit infrared light beyond the visible spectrum for humans but is detectable by the camera's infrared sensors. The camera then processes that information and translates it into a visible image that the camera records.

The team was fully aware of the argument that the orbs we filmed might result from a phenomenon called backscatter, where small dust particles are too close for the lens of the camera to focus on, producing an orb-like image.[2] Viewers will have to judge for themselves if this was the case inside the adobe homestead. Interestingly, both Tom Dongo and Linda Bradshaw strongly believed that the orbs they captured on cameras and reproduced in their books were not the result of backscatter. However, the footage of the light outside the window that synced up with Alan could not have been produced by backscatter since it was in focus as a sharp point of light.

Figure 24: Night Vision Reveals SLS Kinect Infrared Mapping on Alan

Figure 25: Patterson-Gimlin Picture of Bigfoot

With the experiment over, the team packed up our equipment and returned to Sedona. On the way, Ron remembered that a few days earlier, Juergen had taken a picture of what he believed was the best Bigfoot image ever recorded since the iconic Patterson-Gimlin footage.

When Juergen showed Alan the picture, Alan excitedly replied, "That's what I saw!"

At this point, it was clear to the team that we needed to return to the ranch for another round of investigations and experiments. But it would have to wait until next March and the arrival of spring.

Figure 26: Juergen Hess Image of Bigfoot

---

1. All professional video cameras in the 21st century have a night vision mode that can be turned on with the flip of a switch or the push of a button. Each camera uses a video chip, the same as in a gaming computer, which processes night vision footage in black and white because a human's eyes can perceive black and white images better than colors, such as red or blue.
2. In videography backscatter, also known as near-camera reflection, is an optical phenomenon resulting in circular objects captured on the video because of the camera's infrared light reflected from dust, water drops, or other particles in the air close to the camera's lens. When this happens, the camera is unable to focus on the particles and they appear as white blobs.

6

THE SECOND TRIP

After reviewing the footage of our first visit, it was clear that Bradshaw Ranch had much more to offer than we ever anticipated. We now needed to produce a full-length feature film. We had several months to plan our spring trip to Bradshaw Ranch. Spring weather in Northern Arizona's high desert is a mishmash of warm, balmy days and cold rain and snow. But preparing for the weather was a simple matter of packing the appropriate clothing. Our field equipment, on the other hand, needed to become more scientific. In preparation for the second trip to Bradshaw, we decided to update our investigatory toolkit significantly.

Because of our success with the Android GhostTube SLS camera app on Alan's phone, we decided to purchase the real deal—a custom-built Structured Light Sensor (SLS) Kinect Camera.[1]

The SLS camera is based on a device engineered for Microsoft's Xbox series. The Kinect's IR depth sensor projects thousands of tiny infrared dots onto objects and surfaces within its view. By measuring the time these dots take to bounce back, the Kinect can calculate the distance between the sensor and the object, creating a depth map. The software processes this depth map to recognize a player's body movements, gestures, and even facial expressions, allowing them to interact with games and applications without needing a physical controller. As a result, the Xbox Kinect turns the player of the game into an avatar in the game. It's like a moving selfie. The SLS Kinect camera looks out into the world for human-like forms that manifest as avatars from another domain to interact with us.

Figure 27: Structured Light Sensor (SLS) Kinect Camera and Monitor

In addition, SLS Kinect camera has a built-in video camera, a microphone for recording audio, and the ability to convert the image into a display on an attached tablet. The whole apparatus is mounted on a pistol grip. In some ways, the gear is rather Frankensteinian and can be clumsy to handle.

Next, we purchased a portable battery-powered Tesla coil. Tesla coils produce a powerful magnetic field while at the same time releasing free electrons and positive ions.

A growing body of evidence has shown that for alien entities to manifest in our world, they need to draw upon energy from the surrounding environment. It had been suggested that a Tesla coil would provide an ideal energy source for interdimensional entities to manifest.

We also upgraded to the handheld, TriField EMF Meter, Model

TF2. This meter detects two levels of magnetic fluctuation as well as EMF radiation in the radiofrequency range.

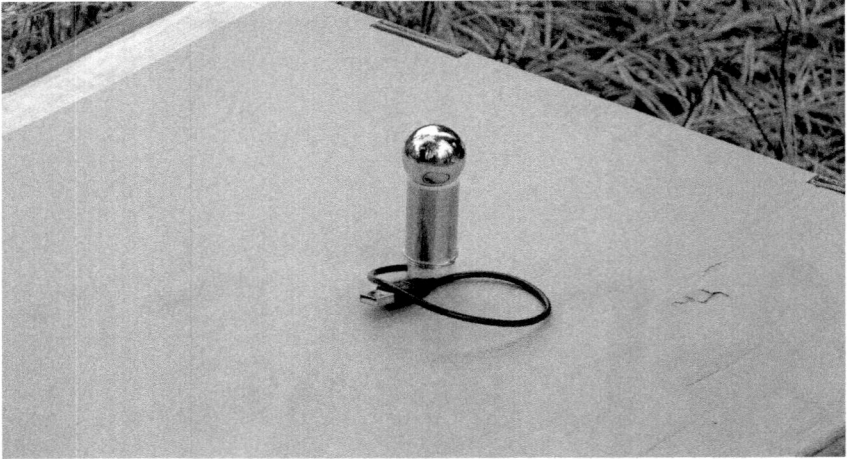

Figure 28: Tesla coil

Finally, we bought a handheld green light laser pointer, which we hoped would allow us to interact nonverbally with an alien entity as Melinda Leslie did with the UAP's.

In addition to our technology upgrade, we employed Benjamin's Lonetree's custom-built, powerful magnetometer and data processing equipment to capture evidence of portals and interdimensional beings.

We now felt ready to explore Bradshaw Ranch for a second time and conduct significant scientific experiments to establish the ranch as a paranormal hotspot comparable to Skinwalker Ranch. What happened was beyond our wildest imagination.

---

1. Since Android-based phones do not have the night vision function, for our second visit we bought a Structured Light Sensor (SLS) Kinect Camera which projects an infrared laser grid over a field of view and shows everything as dots arranged in 3D formation. These infrared dots allow the camera to show depth and detail. The software "sees" people or objects only visible as heat signatures by recognizing joints and movements. The IR will detect paranormal entities that the program recognizes as a human shape based on the body parts and joints.

7

A MOST REMARKABLE SEQUENCE OF SYNCHRONICITIES

W e picked the first weekend in March for our second trip to Bradshaw ranch. The three days would include filming, experiments, and interviews. This particular weekend was chosen because it coincided with CJ Mulkerrin's annual trip to Sedona. We wanted her psychic ability on our team, since she was the person who alerted us to Bradshaw Ranch's paranormal activities. In addition, sensitive Anna Megargle joined us. The plan was to arrive Friday evening and meet with Juergen Hess, who now worked a regular job at one of the many New Age crystal shops in Sedona. His availability was limited to Sunday this weekend, but he confirmed that electrical engineer Benjamin Lonetree would join us and bring his specialized equipment for Sunday night's big experiment. We would be on our own for Saturday.

Because we had decided to make a full-length feature film, it was necessary to do Melinda Leslie's second interview on Saturday morning. She had a long history with the ranch, with the property's earlier investigators and her personal visits. Most importantly, she told us during the interview, "Out at Bradshaw, I have experienced energy fields, and there's one area where if you were to enter that spot, it'll make your hair stand on end, like there's an electric charge. Now, there's nothing out there giving off electricity. I would say the spot is between the ranch house and the adobe homestead. If you walk into it, you will feel this charge. I've been out there when I felt like I was walking into it, but it comes and goes."

Figure 29: Paranormal Investigator Melinda Leslie Discussing the Energy field at Bradshaw Ranch

Saturday morning, after Melinda Leslie's interview concluded, we headed out to the ranch to do more film pickups in each of the two buildings. We also decided to set up two trail cams and return later that night to see what our SLS Kinect camera might reveal.

The hour-long trip to the ranch started off uneventful. However, a sequence of synchronicities began to play out. The events began innocuously enough with a phone call Ron had with CJ on Friday night to work out how she would join the team. It was agreed that she would join us Sunday morning to see the rock art. During the conversation, CJ casually mentioned she had rented a light blue Jeep.

As the team drove toward Bradshaw, Ron spotted a jeep matching CJ's description driving on the gravel road from the ranch. Turning around, we raced to catch up with her. CJ was as surprised as we were that our paths would cross on a lonely stretch of road that is seldom used. She introduced three other psychics she had brought to the ranch and related the harrowing experience she just had while walking on the property.

Figure 30: Producer Ron Meyer with Psychics Janelle Sparkman and CJ Mulkerrin Beside Blue Jeep

"At first, we walked around the adobe homestead, and I did it counterclockwise, and when I came around, all of a sudden, I got hit with this energy, and I felt like I was on fire, like it was burning in my abdomen area. I became dizzy and bent over because I got nauseated. That was enough, so we all decided to leave."

Curiously, CJ's experience matched Melinda Leslie's own experience with the ranch's anomalous spot. Even more strangely, when CJ told Juergen about her episode, he said he knew the spot well. "It can make divining rods go crazy," he explained.

Realizing this would be an important story to film for the movie, Ron asked CJ if she would be willing to go back and show us where the spot was. Much discussion followed with the other three psychics. The four women were uneasy and somewhat hesitant to return to Bradshaw. As one declared, "There's alien technology there." However, they agreed and followed the team back to the property.

In many ways, this improbable coincidence of events was the most remarkable of the synchronicities that occurred during the entire investigation. What were the chances Leslie would offer up the story of this paranormal spot on the ranch. What were the chances that CJ would tell Ron about her light blue Jeep? What were the chances of meeting on the road to the ranch? What were the chances that CJ would experience a phenomenon similar to what Melinda Leslie described in the interview?

Figure 31: Aerial Shot of the Space of High Strangeness Between the Adobe Homestead and Ranch House

Finally, it seemed as if this string of improbable events was necessary in order to lead the team to the most profound experiment, revealing strong evidence of an interdimensional portal on Bradshaw Ranch. This site on the property we would name in the film 'The Space of High Strangeness.'

8

THE SPACE OF HIGH STRANGENESS

Arriving on the property, CJ took us directly to where she had doubled over. The area fit perfectly with the spot Leslie had described her interview earlier that morning. Once again, CJ felt a sense of unease and backed away.

The team experienced nausea and even worse symptoms after our encounter at the space of high strangeness. The phenomenon of 'sizzling' is well-known to some scientists. Dr. Hein later explained, "Some of these energy fields are just not harmonious with our biology. It's something to watch out for, because people who have been exposed without any sort of protection on a long-term basis notice negative biological effects. I imagine you were feeling the first indications of that."

The effect on everyone by the energy field was universal except for our camera operator, Joel Meyer-England, who seemed not to be affected at all. Months later, we still don't know for certain what caused the sizzling, whether it was an electric field as described by Leslie—which would have been impossible since no power lines or electrical power generating equipment was located anywhere on the property—or whether the energy field emanated from a dimension whose physics are slightly different than energy fields formed by our own universe.

Aside from the sizzling, we encountered another problem. From a filmmaker's point of view, the site was unspectacular, with nothing of real interest. We faced an open space on an old trail that connected the two buildings. However, Ron thought that we should see if anything was going on that was not visible to the naked eye.

The team powered up the Tesla coil about twenty feet away from the space of high strangeness. Next, Alan brought out the TriField meter to check for any radio frequency anomalies. He recorded nothing unusual. However, when he scanned for magnetic disturbances, the meter showed the highest level of magnetic flux density on the device's **Gauss display.**

Figure 32: **Alan at the Space of High Strangeness Holding TriField Meter Demonstrating High Magnetic Fluctuation**

The reading shocked all of us. Gauss units measure the strength and direction of a magnetic field at a particular point in space. As Alan said, "This is super unusual. I'm just standing out here in the middle of nothing. No power anywhere, and this meter is going crazy. It's coming and going in waves."

The field Alan detected appeared to be circular and floated over the ground just above his head. The thought that we might be mapping a portal suggested that our next step was verifying the anomalous field using our handheld infrared thermal camera. Immediately, Alan noticed a huge cold spot right in front of us. "It almost looks eyeball-shaped. There is a hot circle that looks like it's jumping around within the cold shape." Alan beckoned over the camera operator, and we were able to film not only the cold spot but a white object moving within it.

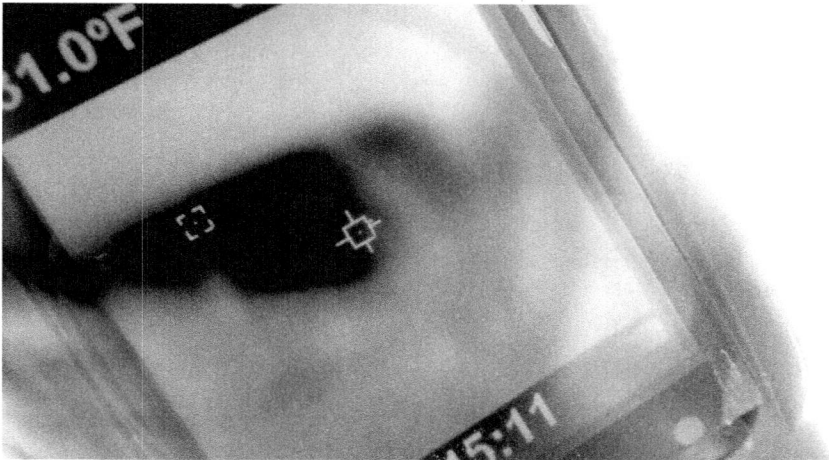

Figure 33:Thermal Device Showing Charged Particle in the Cold Spot at the Space of High Strangeness

The thermal camera also provided a readout of the ambient temperature, which on this spring morning was in the low sixties. However, the cold spot was fluctuating between 18°F and 30°F. Alan walked out on the path between the two buildings and indicated for the camera the phenomenon was about eight feet in the air.

Shortly after showing where the anomaly was floating, Alan checked the area with the TriField meter again, and the phenomenon disappeared. At the same time, everyone was getting a little uneasy.

After letting us know she would join the team the next morning to visit the area's indigenous people's rock art, CJ and her friends said goodbye. They laughingly made jokes about the 'hitchhiker effect'

41

and not bringing the paranormal home with them, but there was no mistaking the concerns they had over what they had just witnessed and felt at Bradshaw.[1]

Figure 34: Alan Indicating the Location of the Potential Interdimensional Portal in the Space of High Strangeness

Before we left the ranch, Alan set up two trail cams. One faced north across the space of high strangeness. The other one looked out upon Juergen Hess's Bigfoot gifting site on the far west side of the property.

Figure 35: Alan Setting up the Trail Cam

Meanwhile, Ron and the camera operator, Joel Meyer-England, did pickups in the adobe homestead and the ranch house to get better coverage of the buildings' interiors to tell the story of the ranch for the film.

By the time the team was back in Sedona, Alan and Ron were feeling crappy. Alan curled up in the fetal position for three hours. Ron's shoulder ached with intense pain. Nevertheless, Ron, Alan, and the camera operator decided to head back to the ranch and try out the new SLS Kinect camera. What showed up was, perhaps, entities that used the portal to visit Bradshaw Ranch. However, the full meaning of what the team had filmed had to wait until we returned home and could look at the footage.

We asked Dr. Hein his opinion of what we had experienced. "Everything in it is going to seem shifted from our point of view. You're going to get temporal anomalies. So it's not surprising that within that space, you saw a charged particle bouncing around in there. That's an indication that you have charged clusters operating at Bradshaw."

Charged clusters are studied in plasma physics and astrophysics. They refer to groups of atoms or molecules with an overall electrical charge. These clusters can be either positively or negatively charged. They are used to understand and manipulate the properties of nano-materials. In nanotechnology, charged clusters are used to engineer novel materials with specific properties. In medicine, they have potential applications in drug delivery and medical imaging. If the clusters are negatively charged, in other words, they are made up of electrons, that would explain Leslie's feeling of entering an electrical field.

It's also been speculated that charged clusters are connected to the opening and closing of interdimensional portals. With this idea in mind, Dr. Hein's hypotheses made sense, and we were drawn to ask the central question that lay at the heart of the paranormal activities observed at Bradshaw Ranch: Had we documented the opening of the interdimensional portal allowing alien entities to move into our universe?

But there's one more synchronicity to the story—setting up the trail camera looking across the space of high strangeness. Later in the editing suite back in Colorado, when we looked at the hundreds of clips recorded by the trail cam, the most interesting phenomenon that occurred was when day shifted to night. A perfect pyramid-shaped triangle showed up over the space of high strangeness. At sunrise the next morning, the pyramid-shaped triangle disappeared.

Figure 36: Triangular Phenomenon over the Space of High Strangeness

Our trail cam uses a Passive Infrared sensor (PIR) that detects heat and motion. At night, the camera throws out an infrared LED illumination, which is reflected back by objects to the camera's infrared sensors. In general, hotter objects appear whitish, and colder objects are darker. Interestingly, although the pyramid is darker, it is also translucent as it is possible to see objects silhouetted behind it.

Saturday night at Bradshaw Ranch, the most astonishing event captured by the trail cam was a swarm of hundreds of softball-sized white circular objects rapidly pouring out of the ground and the triangle.

Figure 37: Softball-Sized White Orbs Pouring out of the Triangular Phenomenon

These objects could not have been attributed to backscatter in front of the camera's lens, especially since the grass close to the lens was perfectly still. Then, when viewing the second to last shot on Sunday night, the balls of light disappeared back into the triangle. In addition, a similar swarm of objects passed behind the windmill in the distance in one of the trail cam's other clips.

Figure 38: Swarm of UAPS Passing Behind Bradshaw Ranch Windmill

Sometime later, Ron showed the screen grab of the pyramid to Seth Feinstein, a Mutual UFO Network video forensic expert. Seth immediately identified the triangle as an interdimensional portal.

Upon reflection, it seemed that the long sequence of synchronicities leading to our filming at Bradshaw Ranch could have had a singular purpose. Was it possible we were intentionally drawn to Bradshaw to show the world that the charged clusters pouring out of the triangle were some kind of alien beings as Tom Dongle believed? Furthermore, was it possible that the entities we captured on our SLS Kinect camera were these alien beings?

Finally, once back in Colorado, we tested the trail cam under several nighttime scenarios to see if we could reproduce the triangle effect. Our efforts met with no success. In fact, we had used the camera before and since our second trip to Bradshaw Ranch with no such lens anomaly.

---

1. The 'Hitchhiker Effect'—also known as the 'Skinwalker Ranch Hitchhiker Effect'—refers to the sometimes-terrifying paranormal effects that occur at home after visiting a paranormal site, such as Bradshaw Ranch. Experiencers feel as though a paranormal effect has attached itself to them and 'hitchhiked' back to their homes. Paranormal hitchhikers can include shadow beings, electrical anomalies, objects thrown around the house and blue orbs inside and outside the home.

9

THE SLS KINETIC CAMERA REVEALS ENTITIES

The temperature dropped considerably when the team arrived at Bradshaw Saturday night. The first thing we did was to see if there were any anomalous readings in the space of high strangeness. Probing with the TriField Meter and the thermal camera showed the same normal readings as earlier in the afternoon. This was evidence supporting the hypothesis that portals open and close.

Our next step was to try the SLS Kinect Camera. One of the SLS camera's drawbacks is that visible light overwhelms the infrared output during daylight hours, rendering the camera ineffective. But now that it was night, we searched the space of high strangeness. As we suspected, nothing showed up on the screen.

People who have seen the movie have asked, "Were you disappointed that dramatic readings and physiological effects at the space of high strangeness apparently disappeared?"

We were not. Serious investigators and filmmakers of the paranormal, the anomalous, and the impossible are aware that, almost by definition, these events have to be one-time happenings. Paraphrasing John Keel, one of the founding fathers of modern paranormal investigations, The 'it' will show you something, but 'it' will not perform for you. Keel said in his most famous statement, "If you start studying 'it', 'it' will start studying you." Following Keel's guidance, we practiced being open to the next unexpected event and hoped we would be able to capture 'it' on film.[1]

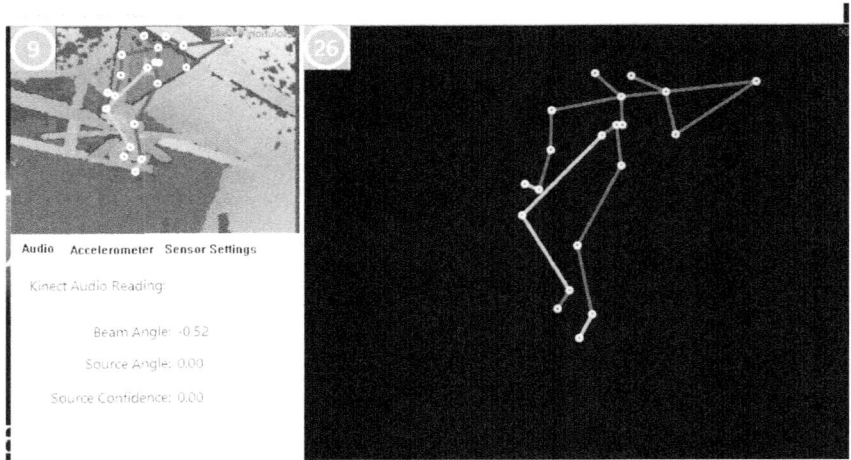

Figure 39: Amorphous Stick Figure Near Ceiling in Adobe Homestead

And we were not disappointed when we entered the adobe homestead with the SLS Kinect camera in hand. When Alan entered the smaller room, an amorphous stick figure appeared on the monitor near the ceiling. Alan began recording. The figure did not have a human shape, and it appeared to be moving erratically.[2]

Moments later, the figure vanished. Alan turned to the camera operator and said, "That's weird when it just disappears." He then continued scanning the room, but nothing else showed up.

We next moved into the larger room, where Alan had his Bigfoot experience on our first visit to Bradshaw Ranch. When the camera operator and Alan were ready, Ron turned on his green light laser pointer, and something amazing happened. Alan, once more pointing the SLS Kinect camera towards the ceiling, observed, "Look at that... Two things up by the beam." This time, the SLS stick figures were more humanoid, though they still appeared to be dancing while at the same time popping into and out of existence.

Next, Ron, having seen where the entities showed up, pointed his laser at the place where the entities appeared, and Alan began recording. Immediately, another entity showed up and reached for the laser beam. This reaction was more than we could have hoped for. It showed the entity possessed awareness of the laser beam and moved to touch it, demonstrating purposeful behavior. As with the other two entities, this one disappeared suddenly. Looking at the playback, we were relieved to see we got everything on camera. Paranormal investigative teams have experienced cameras inexplicably failing when filming the paranormal.

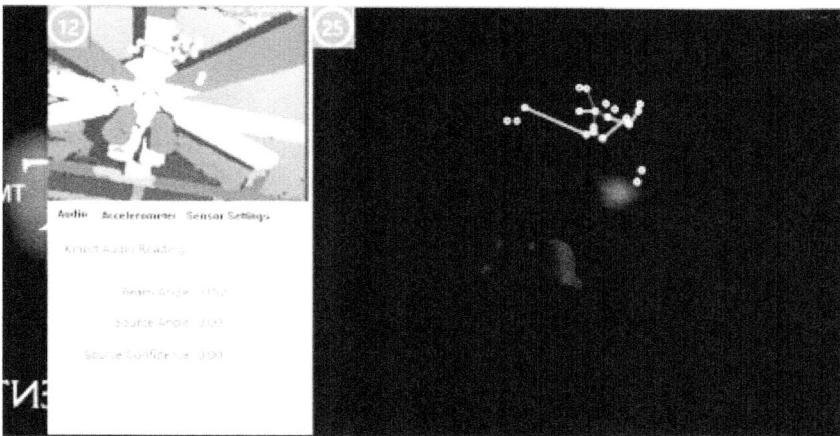

Figure 40: Entity Touching Laser in Big Room, Adobe Homestead

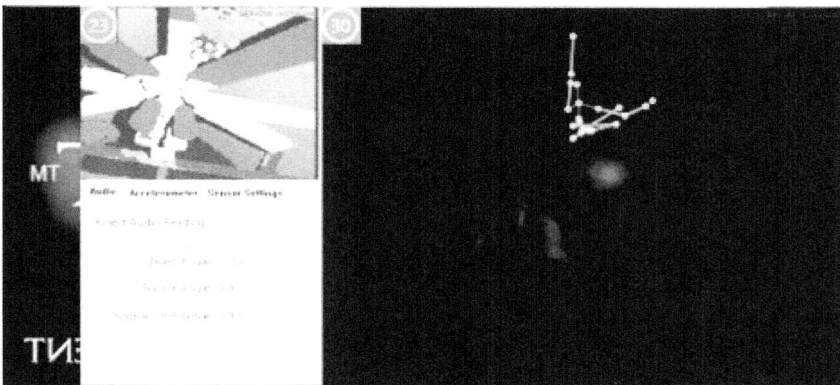

Figure 41: Entity Touching Laser in Big Room Adobe Homestead

Next, we moved to the ranch house. Upon entering, a loud bang reverberated throughout the building, reminding us of a Bigfoot wood knock. "A good sign," we joked. "Maybe there's a Bigfoot lurking inside."

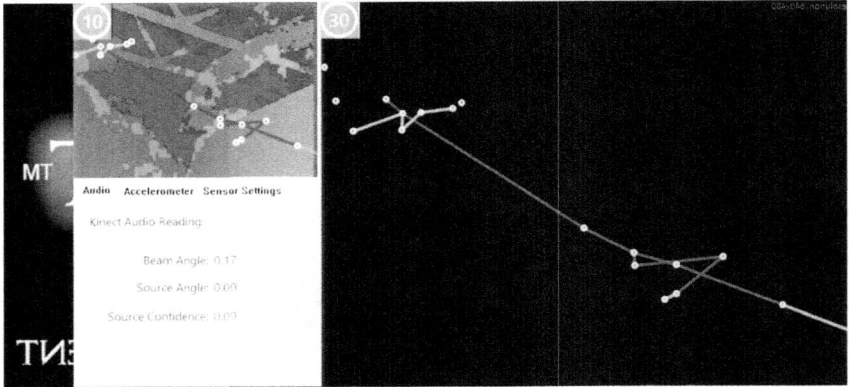

Figure 42: Entity in Ranch House Near Ceiling

While walking from room to room, scanning with the SLS camera, suddenly, another non-humanoid entity appeared above our heads near the ceiling. This one spanned quite a distance and was also in dancing mode.

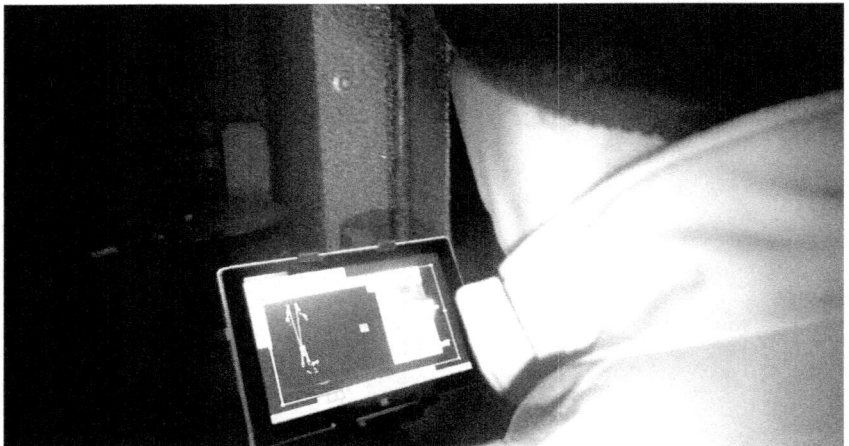

Figure 43a: Entity in Ranch House Main Room Leaping to the Ceiling

50

Moving to the main room, Ron turned on his green light laser. As if on cue, two dancing, amorphous images appeared on the SLS camera's screen, then disappeared just as quickly. A few minutes later, one more non-human life form appeared, this time closer to the floor. We watched it rise and disappear into the ceiling a few moments later.

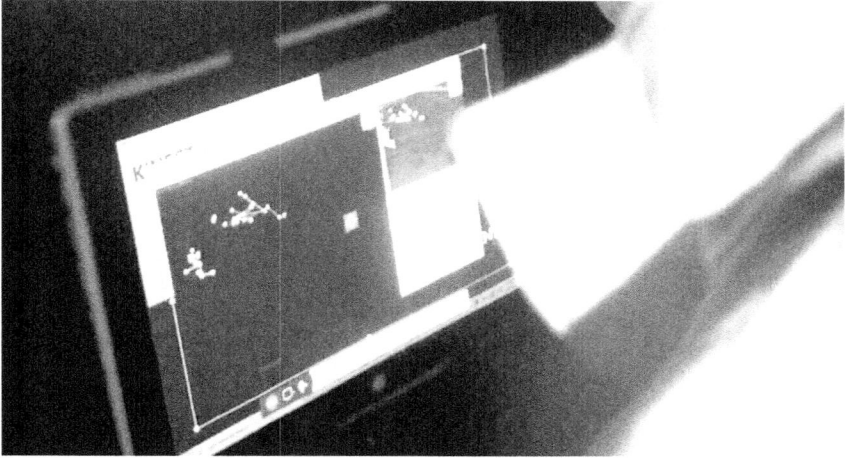

Figure 43b: Entities in Ranch House Main Room Apparently Dancing

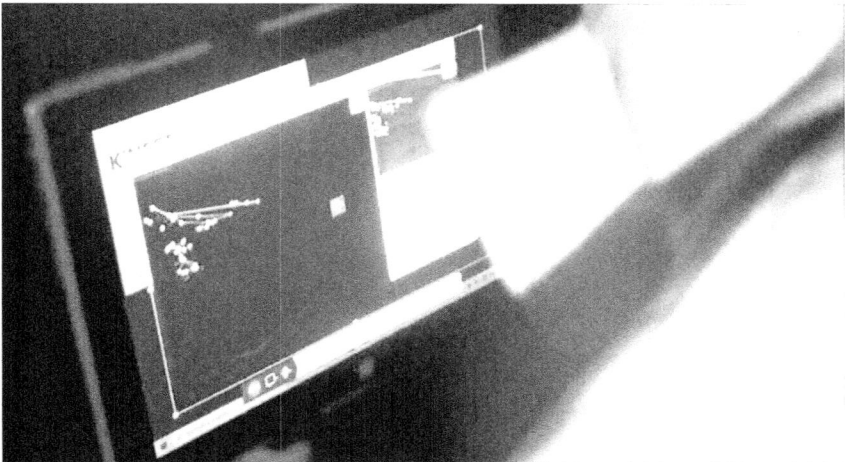

Figure 43c: Entities in Ranch House Main Room Apparently Dancing

Exhilarated by what we had captured on film, we decided the ranch house's main room would be where we would conduct our final experiment Sunday night. We returned to Sedona and much needed rest. Sunday would be an adventure-filled day. In the morning, Juergen Hess planned to show the team some astonishing Native American rock art panels. Later that night, our defining experiment with Benjamin Lonetree's special equipment would occur.

---

1. Keel and other paranormal researchers are not trying to be clever or humorous or misleading with the term 'it'. When probing the paranormal, researchers need to keep an open mind about what they will uncover or be exposed to. Entering an investigation with a preconceived idea of what one will find, ultimately influences the outcome. Known as Observer Bias, this circumstance occurs when a researcher's expectations, opinions, or prejudices influence what they perceive or record in a study. For example, if our team at Bradshaw Ranch looked upon the entities we observed as originating from some interdimensional civilization, we would of necessity and carelessly view and interpret these entities in terms of human civilization, which would be misleading not only to readers and film viewers but to the scientific method: systematic observation, measurement, and experiment, and the formulation, testing, and modification of hypotheses.

2. An annoying feature of the SLS Kinect camera is that it can produce an artifact that makes objects on the screen appear as though dancing. This particular effect is caused by air movement and temperature changes between the camera and the object being captured.

10

ANCESTRAL PUEBLOAN ROCK ART

Irst thing Sunday morning, we met Juergen Hess for a trip deep into the northern Arizona high desert close to Bradshaw Ranch. Juergen had agreed to guide us to the secret rock art panels created by the ancient Sinagua Indians. Ancestors of the contemporary Hopi and Zuni Puebloan people, the Sinagua inhabited the forests, canyons, grasslands, and deserts of central and northern Arizona from about A.D. 600 through A.D. 1450. Like their contemporaries, the Anasazi to the east, the Sinagua built Pueblo dwellings and lived a rich spiritual life often represented in their rock art, known as petroglyphs and pictographs.

Petroglyphs are rock carvings made by pecking directly on the rock surface using a stone chisel and a hammerstone. When the surface of the rock's dark desert varnish is pecked off, the lighter layers beneath are exposed, creating the art images. Pictographs are drawings or illustrations created from pigments made from natural sources, such as ochres and iron oxides, found in the surrounding landscape.

The amazing rock art panels created by the Sinagua people are a guide to a universe greater than our own. In fact, the Sinagua people, through their rock art and oral traditions, told tales of regular contact with visitors they named Star Beings. Moreover, the Sinagua referred to these visitors as their Star Ancestors.

Figure 44: Petroglyph with Distinctive Patina from Weathering

Figure 45: Sego Canyon, Utah, Pictograph with Red Ochre

Juergen led the team through scrub brush and desert to the red sandstone cliffs used as a canvas to portray what the Sinagua people felt the need to immortalize. The cliffs run along the far side of a normally dry creek. However, the day we visited, the creek was filled with a raging torrent that made access all but impossible. After much discussion, Juergen and our camera operator, Joel Meyer-England, agreed to cross the turbulent river and make the difficult and treacherous climb to the rock cliffs.

The first panel Juergen showed us possibly represented a human entering a portal or vortex. The inward-moving spiral—something that goes back to the ancient Egyptians—is an opening to another dimensional world from which aliens move through to our plane of existence.

Tom Dongo's good friend, the Santee Shaman, Jim White, whose Dakota name is Waykiniipicye, meaning Moves Like Thunder, interprets these spirals to mean that the Star People arrived for the singular purpose of changing the people living in the area at the time.

"Life is going to change for those people and those animals at that place and time," Waykiniipicye explained. A person viewing the rock art of his ancestors, then, would be linked to the past through this spiral or vortex and know that his or her life had been changed by the Star Beings who arrived in this area tens of thousands of years ago as described in the Sinagua's oral traditions.

Figure 46: Juergen Hess with Sinagua Spiral/Vortex Petroglyph

Figure 47: Sinagua Petroglyph of Bigfoot Holding up Deer

Next, we saw a panel depicting humans surrounding a Bigfoot who has grabbed the leg of a deer. It appears as if the Bigfoot is hunting. However, perhaps it is not hunting just for himself but also for the humans.

This interpretation fits with the altruistic nature of Bigfoot as experienced by Waykiniipicye. The Santee Shaman describes Bigfoot as *Sitanka* or big brothers. One particular Bigfoot would appear at his ceremonies, and when he asked the Bigfoot to help people on the reservation who needed help, the Bigfoot would go help them. In his own words, Waykiniipicye described the Bigfoot as, "Intelligence, it's relative and it's a helper. I don't see it as a creature or a flesh-eating monster." He added, "There's different tribes that live in all different parts of the world. The ones around here seem to be real calm."

Finally, Juergen showed us a petroglyph only reachable on the sheer cliffs by the camera's long lens. Hidden away on this panel is the most remarkable rock art. The image shows what appears to be the classical outline of a saucer-shaped UFO flying above people, possibly in a worshiping position, looking up at the craft.

Waykiniipicye believes this drawing depicts an actual happening among the Sinagua. He interprets it as, "They are looking in the sky, and they see this thing, this craft, but at the same time, maybe they came from it, too, and they are remembering."

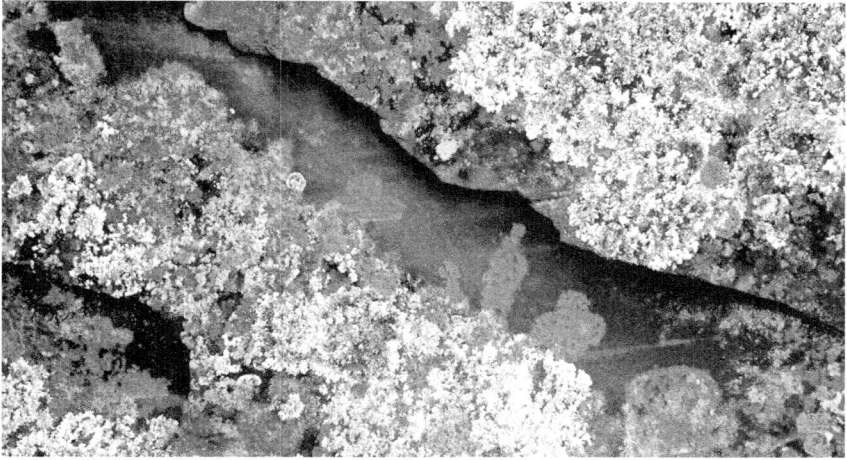

Figure 48: Sinagua Petroglyph of People Seeing a UFO

Why these ancestral indigenous people would go to the trouble of creating these puzzling yet insightful drawings in out-of-the-way places appears on the surface to be a mystery. But the paranormal and mystical ambiance of America's Desert Southwest presupposes a more rigorous and compelling reason.

Santee Shaman Waykiniipicye cleared up some of that mystery for us. "The relatives drew drawings like that ... one was to identify who they were, identify other things around them such as UFOs, Bigfoot, animals, even the spirals. What I believe is they used it. They recorded it in that way so that they would always remember that. But at the same time, what I also believe is that when they ascend into the star camps, they are leaving something there for the new ones that are coming, sometimes they say reincarnation, and it gives them an identity to survive on this planet. So, I believe it serves several different purposes. It's a recording of history, and at the same time, it is almost like a map. Your soul leaves and comes back again, and it remembers that place and that scenario, and that way, it helps it not to be lost."

We write in Appendix C that the oral traditions related by Native Americans are more than myths or wishful thinking or legends. And so it is also in these amazing petroglyphs we filmed. Indeed, each one of the rock art panels we encountered echoes a non-human or super-human intelligence. A sentiment shared by every Native American people in the Four Corners region. A sentiment depicted in their art and transmitted orally in their creation stories.

When Juergen and the camera operator returned from their adventure filming these amazing rock art panels, the rest of us immediately wanted to see what they had filmed. When Joel showed us the image of the UFO, it put us in a wonderful frame of mind for what we would experience for the rest of the time at Bradshaw Ranch.

11

BENJAMIN LONETREE ARRIVES

S light of build and full of energy, Benjamin Lonetree is a retired electrical engineer and master builder of powerful electronic devices when he worked for the federal government and other agencies. When the main film crew arrived Sunday afternoon, following lunch, for our final experiment, Benjamin was already on site with Juergen. As promised, he had brought the special system he had designed for detecting and studying the geomagnetic anomalies—reported by the US geological survey—found at Sedona's world-renowned red rock mesas.

Benjamin Lonetree described these geomagnetic anomalies, known locally as vortexes. "The vortexes emit a very intense spiraling magnetic field of energy. And I've actually recorded that magnetic field spiraling. So, it's real." In addition, he speculated that the vortexes were a result of non-dipole magnetism periodically spinning up from magnetic activity below the Earth's crust and then reconnecting back to the ground, returning to its natural dipole state on the mesas' surfaces.

As to the vortex's purported spiritual and health benefits, Benjamin believes they alter a person's state of consciousness, making them more susceptible to otherwise undetectable energy forces.

Figure 49: Left to Right: Ron Meyer, Alan Megargle, Benjamin Lonetree and Juergen Hess at Bradshaw Ranch

Benjamin's research has also demonstrated that the whole area around Sedona, including Bradshaw Ranch, has elevated magnetic and positive ion spikes erupting from below earth. He speculates, "If you look at all the red rock sandstone this is a result of iron oxide, commonly known as rust. Iron oxide is inductive electronically, and when you add a quartz layer below the sandstone layer, that is a formula for generating electricity. As a result, intermittently, positive ions, electricity, and magnetic energy are released into the space above the ground. Consequently, this whole area can open interdimensional portals, allowing crafts, alien entities, and orbs to enter the space here. They come here in a plasma or charged cluster state. They can then manifest in our reality and do whatever they need to do, and then they shimmer back into their plasma or charged cluster state and disappear."

At the heart of the specialized equipment Benjamin brought to the ranch is a powerful custom-built magnetometer. The magnetometer is equipped with state-of-the-art sensors that detect the presence and characteristics of magnetic fields surrounding the device. He described to us the flow of information from the magnetometer to his computer, which records the data. "What we have here is the magnetometer, which sends its output to an electronic conversion box. The signal moves onto a data acquisition module, which then converts the signal to data, which the computer can use to turn the data into a graphical display of the activity generated by the magnetometer."

As we finished filming the interview with Benjamin, CJ Mulkerrin arrived, and we made plans for the nighttime experiment in the ranch house. Benjamin wanted to set up his equipment in the adobe homestead first in order to establish a baseline of the magnetic activity on the ranch. He figured it would take a couple of hours.

Figure 50: Benjamin Lonetree and CJ Mulkerrin Talking Together

This gave Ron, Alan, and Joel enough time to make the trek to Juergen's Bigfoot gifting site on the west end of the property. Our guide wanted to share with us a curious event he had experienced a few days earlier. Along the way we filmed the sophisticated and expensive sensor array described in Chapter Two that some unknown researchers had left behind. We also filmed more extraordinary Bigfoot trackways.

A Bigfoot gifting site is where the researcher hopes to make contact with the creature by exchanging objects. Juergen has had some mild success with a few items, particularly food. But he particularly wanted to show us a simple electronic device made for pets. Using the device's pushbutton controls, a person can record their voice.

Figure 51: Bradshaw Ranch Bigfoot Trackway from Second Visit

Figure 52: Electronic Recording Devices Used by Juergen Hess

Juergen had placed two of the devices on his gifting site. The next day, when he returned, both had recordings on them. One sounded like an animal eating the grapes Juergen had left behind as a gift. The other one, however, had recorded a female or child's voice speaking in an unrecognizable language. Slowed down, the recording sounded like 'ah de seah.' Another Bradshaw mystery for us to film.

Next, Alan removed the trail cam we had set up to capture whatever might enter the gifting site. Someone or something had turned off the trail cam for the second time, leaving us nothing to show the audience.

The trip to the far side of the ranch had taken up most of the late afternoon. We quickly lost light and needed to hurry back to the ranch house for the big experiment. We hoped by the time we returned, Benjamin's equipment would be calibrated and the evening at Bradshaw Ranch would provide something spectacular to film for our movie.

12

THE BIG EXPERIMENT

As darkness settled in, Benjamin moved his equipment from the Adobe homestead into the main room of the ranch house. Luckily, there was a bench along the west wall, near where we had captured stick figures on the SLS Kinect camera the night before.

Figure 53: Benjamin Lonetree with His Equipment in the Ranch House

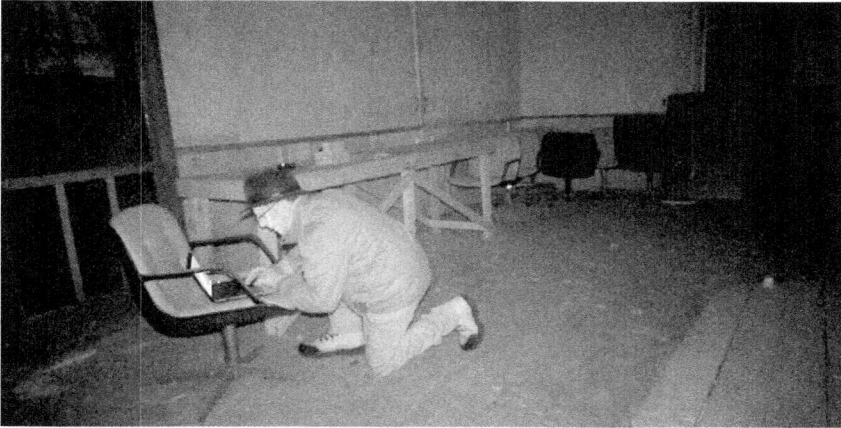

Figure 54: Benjamin Lonetree Moves His Computer to the Chair

Benjamin told us that his system had established a typical Sedona baseline along with the usual intermittent magnetic spikes that arose on the ranch as well. Once the equipment was laid out, Benjamin began to calibrate the system. Immediately, he encountered unexpected resistance, almost as if something were purposefully interfering with his efforts. In an attempt to make it easier to work on the computer, Benjamin moved it onto the seat of a chair left of the bench.

At the same time, Alan fired up the Tesla coil twenty-five feet from Benjamin's setup in order not to interact with his magnetometer. A raised platform with a couple of chairs placed between the bench and the Tesla coil.

The team assembled in the room far enough away from the magnetometer so as not to be picked up by its sensors. For some reason, CJ turned on the SLS app on her iPhone and picked up a remarkable sequence of events shown here in four screen grabs.

Figure 55 shows the computer and an elevated stick figure to the left in a partial humanoid form touching the plasma ball on the top of the Tesla coil.

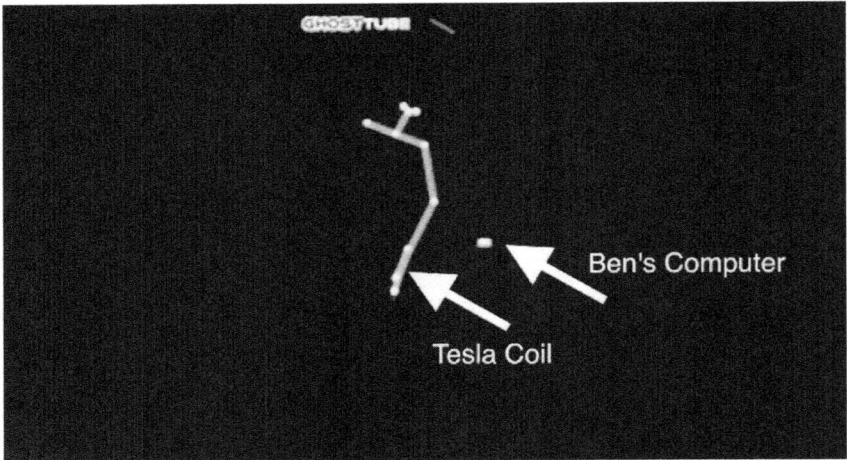

Figure 55: CJ's SLS Image of Entity Touching Tesla Coil

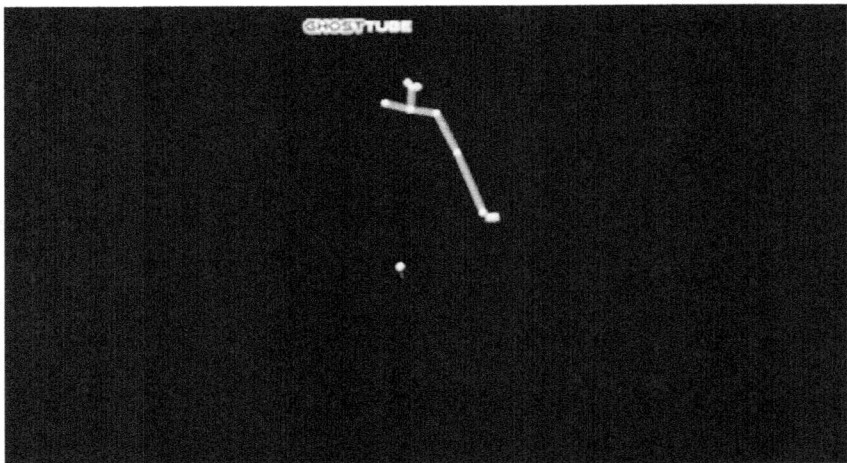

Figure 56: CJ's SLS Image of Entity Touching Computer

This image is followed a few frames later, with the stick figure touching the computer, shown in Figure 56. Shortly after, a fully formed humanoid figure is recorded in Figure 57, touching the computer and the Tesla coil, though they are twenty-five feet apart. In the final screen grab, Figure 58, the stick figure again touches the Tesla coil.

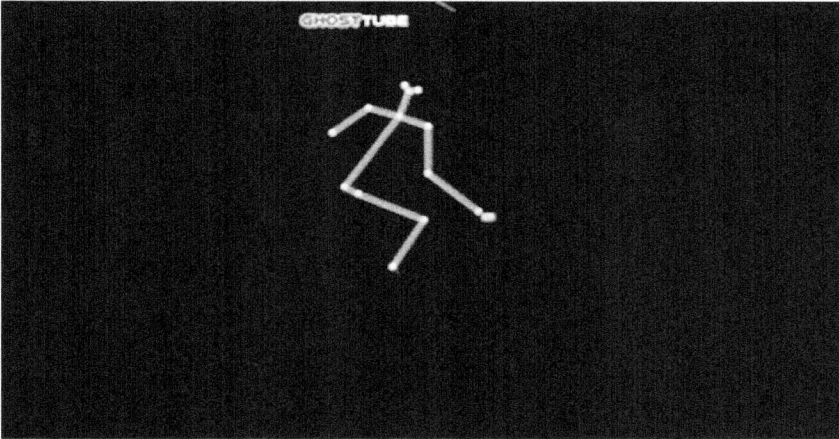

Figure 57: Entity Touching Tesla Coil and Computer

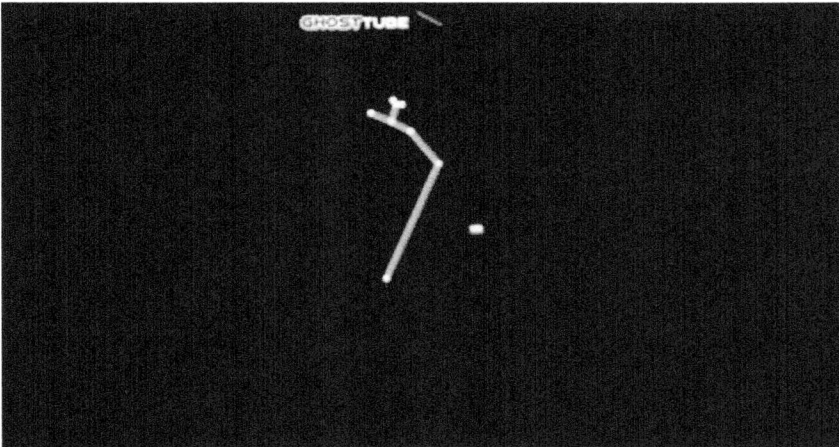

Figure 58: Entity Touching Tesla Coil Again

Watching the movements of the humanoid stick figure, it would be reasonable to speculate that an entity was gathering energy from the Tesla coil to materialize and perform the next actions during our experiment.

Immediately after CJ reported what she saw on her smartphone's SLS app, Alan turned on the SLS Kinect camera and at once captured the humanoid figure above and to the right of Benjamin while he was trying to calibrate his computer.

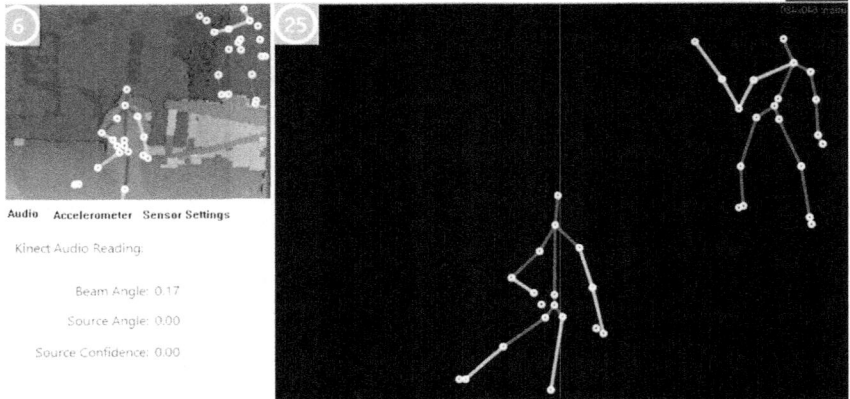

Figure 59: SLS Kinect Camera Captures Entity (above right) and Benjamin Lonetree (bottom center) as Lonetree Struggles with his Computer

At the same time, Benjamin complained that something was fighting him and not allowing him to calibrate his computer.

Later, when Benjamin returned home, he created a frequency spectrum display on his computer screen for the time we had been interacting with the entity. The display, shown below, began with the calibrated baseline produced inside the adobe homestead that showed minor fluctuations arising from the ranch's normal magnetic discharges and positively charged ions.

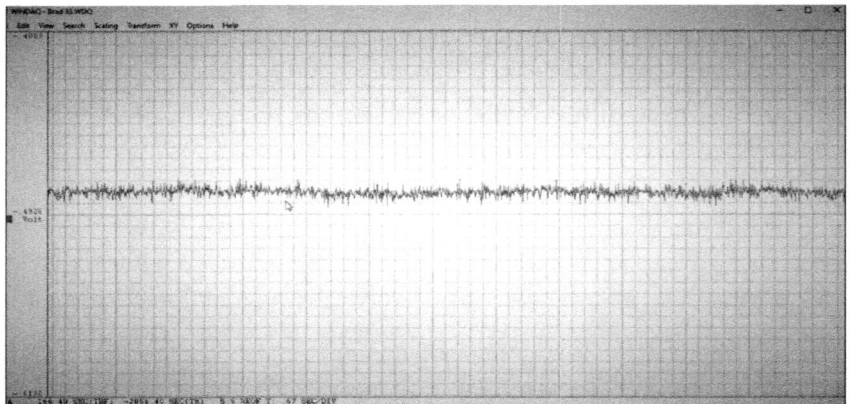

Figure 60: Calibrated Base Line Produced Inside the Adobe Homestead Showing Minor Fluctuations Arising from the Ranch's Normal Magnetic Discharges & Positively Charged Ions

68

The next picture shows what was happening in the ranch house when Benjamin had been trying to calibrate his computer. As you can see, the activity is off the charts. Some of the spikes belong to Benjamin because he's close to the sensor, but the entity produces the rest.

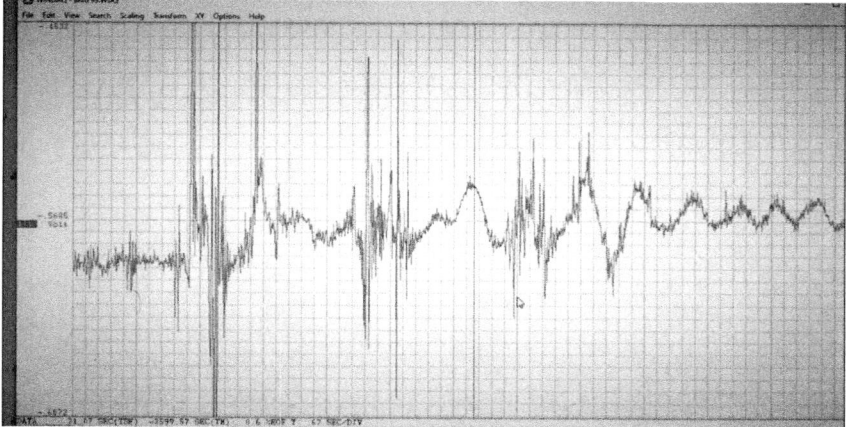

Figure 61: Computer Image of Spikes Caused by Entity

Benjamin then moved away from the computer and the magnetometer and joined the rest of the team about thirty feet away.

Figure 62: Benjamin Standing with Team Away from His Equipment

69

Abruptly, the entity, now fully in a humanoid form, showed up on the SLS Kinect camera, sitting in one of the platform's chairs. The dancing aberration caused by the fluctuating temperature difference between the object and the camera was gone. In addition, the head was definitely looking around as if searching for something.

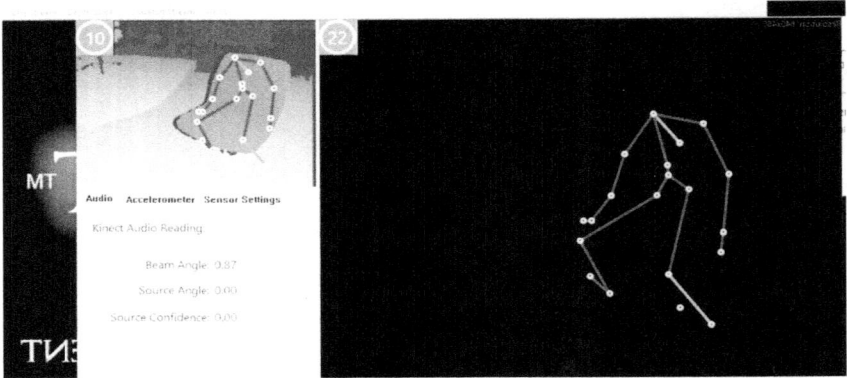

Figure 63: Humanoid Entity Sitting in Platform Chair Sees Laser Beam

Ron pointed his laser at the entity's foot. Immediately, the entity looked down at the laser beam and then clearly kicked at it with its left foot, distinctly demonstrating awareness of the situation. (Figures 64, 65, and 66 show the entity kicking Ron's laser pointer.)

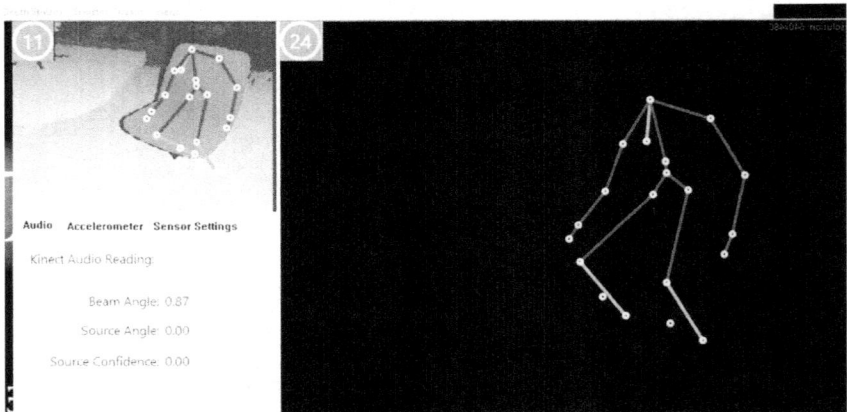

Figure 64: Humanoid Entity Watches as it Begins Kicking at Laser Beam

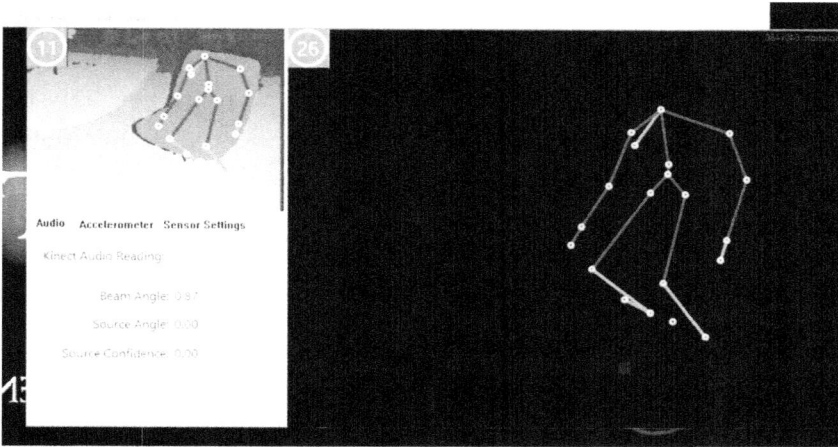

Figure 65: Humanoid Entity Kicking Laser Beam

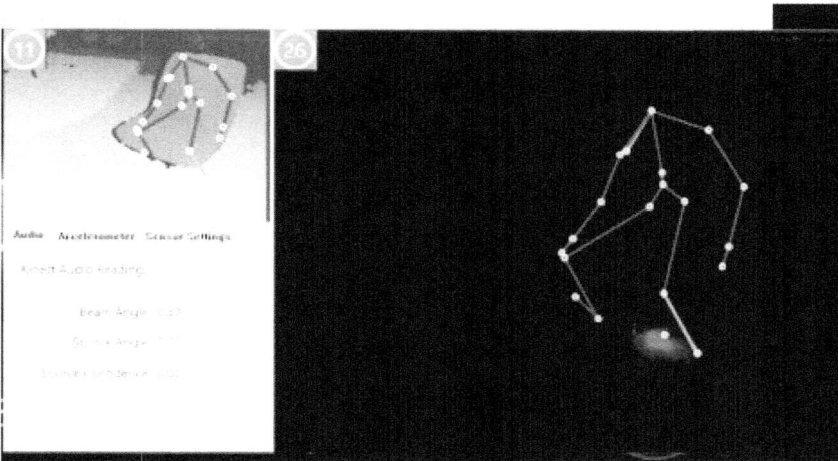

Figure 66: Humanoid Entity Finishes Kicking Laser Beam

Alan showed the team what he had just recorded on his camera. For some reason, Juergen jumped on the platform and sat on the adjacent chair. When Alan pointed his SLS Kinect camera at him, Juergen said, "I feel like I'm bouncing up and down." Then, to everyone's surprise, the entity emerged out of Juergen and flew up toward the ceiling. On the ceiling, it temporarily lost its humanoid form before disappearing.

The team thought the experiment was concluded, but the entity had another surprise for us. The entity emerged from Juergen a second time, flew up to the ceiling, and disappeared. Amazingly, the entity did what most paranormal events never do: repeat themselves. The entity then showed up a third time, sitting in the original chair. It seemed almost as if waiting for something. Juergen responded by going over to the chair and sitting down. However, nothing more happened. The entity was gone and did not return for the next ten minutes.

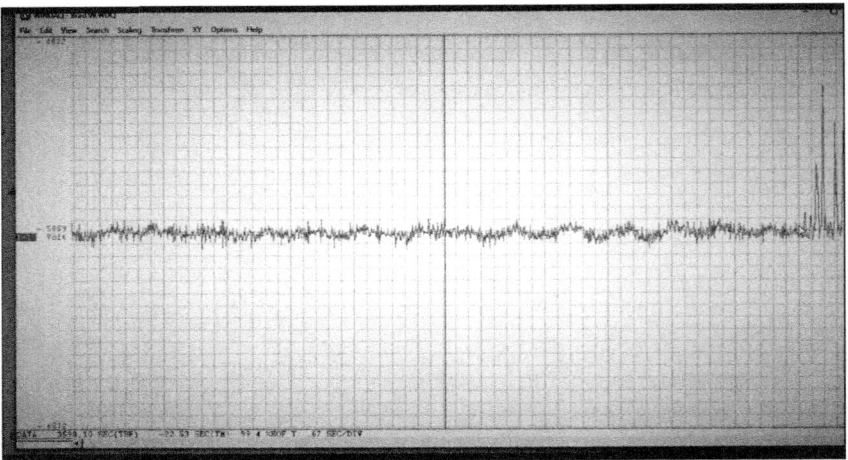

Figure 67: Last Recorded Ion Spike as Entity Disappears (right hand side)

The image above shows what Benjamin calls the waveform signature of the entity. At the same time, his magnetometer also picked up positive ion activity, which Benjamin believes is caused by the opening of the portal that allowed the entity to come into our reality.

Later, according to the waveform, the entity appeared to be back at the computer, and there was a massive sequence of positive spikes before the computer went dead. When Benjamin checked his computer, the batteries had not been drained. The computer had merely been turned off, and when Benjamin restarted it, it worked perfectly. This event begged the question: Did the entity turn off the computer as indicated by the massive positive spike before returning to its reality?

We all went outside to discuss what had just happened. Strangely and yet at the same time, what seemed to be a matter of course with the events of the evening, a black hawk helicopter showed up and flew nearby us. We all shrugged a big 'of course ... the perfect ending to the evening.' We gathered our gear and removed the trail cam, filming the space of high strangeness between the two buildings.

During the whole time of this interaction, Benjamin's equipment gathered enormous amounts of data, recording the entity's interaction with us. While reviewing the computer readout, he said that everything his equipment recorded during our experiment was the entity because he had joined the team standing too far away to be picked up by the magnetometer.

We left Bradshaw, eager to return home and review the footage we had captured. What started out six months ago to be a ten-minute ending to another paranormal film had grown into a full-length feature film, showing the world that we are not alone in the universe. We had documented the strongest evidence so far that Bradshaw Ranch—as many researchers, investigators, and sensitives have claimed—is indeed populated at least from time to time by entities that are aware of us and our technology. Moreover, we had evidence of the existence of an interdimensional portal these entities might have used to reach our world. The movie itself is *The Mysteries of Bradshaw Ranch: Aliens, Portals and the Paranormal*.

CONCLUSIONS

A NOTE FROM THE AUTHORS

As the authors conclude this book on Bradshaw Ranch, it's important to note that investigators continue to perform experiments at the property for its paranormal activities. Indeed, Benjamin Lonetree, successfully duplicated the results of our team's final experiment in the main room-on the last night. In conversation with Ron, Benjamin told him he built a much larger Tesla coil, and as soon as he fired it up, entities appeared on his SLS Kinect camera. One time, he was able to film an alien entity touching a female filmmaker who had come to the ranch, and she was able to feel the touch of the entity. At places like Bradshaw ranch, the veil revealing a greater reality is lifting in two ways.

First, during the lifetime of this book, it can be expected that the U.S. government will reveal more information about UAPs and UFOs being of alien origin, that is, not derived from Earth's biological lineage. A major characteristic of this alien presence will most likely not be an advanced civilization, as humans define civilization and its technology, but as nonhuman intelligences with advanced capabilities. Furthermore, the U.S. government will reveal that alien presences have been around for a very long time.

Second, government and private research will openly support the predictions that when people become more open to talking about their paranormal experiences, sea change will occur. Though inexplicable by consensus science, these experiences are transformational and as more and more people share their stories of high strangeness, a new kind of human will emerge through the process, a human with superpowers.

* * *

Ron Meyer's Thoughts:

As the producer-director of the movie, I could not be more pleased as to how it turned out, in that we were able to film a wide range of paranormal phenomena. ' I believe we've added important evidence and data points regarding answers to these questions: 'Are we alone in the universe?' ... 'Do interdimensional portals exist?'... and 'Is there a more encompassing physics that needs to be created to understand who we are as human beings?'—

On a personal side, I firmly believe something or some entity is aware of me and, at times, has provided what I call a sequence of meaningful synchronicities in the creation and production of my movies depicting the paranormal domain. There is no better example of this phenomenon than in the making of the movie this book is based on.

My biggest job while the investigation team was on-site at Bradshaw Ranch, was to be open to whatever was needed to be done next in order to make meaningful sequences to film. This process was particularly difficult when it came to filming the paranormal because what happened next and then again next, and then again next was never expected. As a result, I often needed a bird's eye perspective of what was going on, and therefore, I was unable to share directly in some of the experiences the investigators were having. Of course, I did have the joy in postproduction when looking at the footage to see things that nobody had directly seen.

Twice, we encountered evidence of what might be interdimensional portals. The first one occurred in the ranch house, where the team experienced the sudden appearance of a column of very cold air with high magnetic fluctuations. The second encounter happened at what we called 'the space of high strangeness.' Magnetic fluctuations peaked our TriField Meter, and when we put our thermal camera on it, we saw a large cold area with a smaller, extremely hot object moving within it.

People have speculated that what we captured was a temporary merging of our reality with another and that the hot object in the center was indeed something manifesting from the other universe.

Several factors during our investigation support this hypothesis. First, our biology, when we entered the space of high strangeness, did not do well. We were in paranormal parlance 'sizzled.'

Then, later, when I reviewed our trail cam footage looking at the space of high strangeness, the camera captured a permanent large triangular shape in the infrared realm over the space of high strangeness. In addition, twice, the trail cam recorded swarms of UAPs pouring out of the triangle and later back into it. These occurrences support the thesis that portals exist as a means for nonhuman intelligences to enter our reality.

Regarding the nonhuman entities we captured with our SLS Kinect camera, I believe this indicates something intelligent at Bradshaw Ranch is aware of us and can interact with us through our technology. Moreover, it seems to be difficult for these intelligences to manifest in a form we can handle.

Finally, it takes energy such as provided by the environment or the Tesla coil, for these entities to appear in our reality, and as a result, the manifestations are short-term. It has been suggested by some investigators that these entities might be essences of people who have died. In other words, coming from another plane of existence. But whatever they are, they are real.

Ron Meyer, January 1st 2024

* * *

Mark Reeder's Thoughts:

What exactly did the investigation uncover? Addressing the question from my historian perspective, I would say the answer is three-fold.

First, it supports my belief that what is most likely a paradigm shift is happening in our fundamental understanding of life outside of earth. Not unlike the Copernican revolution in astronomy, which showed our planet not to be the center of the solar system, Bradshaw Ranch has shown humans are not alone in the vast universe that surrounds planet earth.

Second, as when Einstein, Bohr, and Planck revolutionized Newtonian physics, Bradshaw Ranch is ground zero for developing a paradigm shift to bring physics to a new level of possibilities. As the word paranormal suggests—events or phenomena beyond the scope of normal scientific understanding—so are the events happening at Bradshaw Ranch. They open the door, not unlike the way the 19th century's premier scientist Nikola Tesla opened the door to make 21st century technological marvels such as smartphones and wireless devices possible.

And finally, it appears to me that the 'it' described in Chapter 9 by John Keel is helping to transform humanity from human to superhuman. This is not the Nietzschean ideal of the Ubermensch, as described by Friedrich Wilhelm Nietzsche in *Thus Spake Zarathustra*. Paranormal experiencers are unlikely to become 'the superior man of the future who can rise above conventional Christian morality to create and impose his own values.' Instead, the paranormal experience is a fundamental flowering of human potential open to every person on the planet.

In religious terms, the 21st century message of the paranormal experience is the fulfillment of the teachings of Jesus, Buddha, Mohammed, Lao Tzu, Baha'ulla, Moses, and others. More simply put, once we understand that these paranormal experiences are transformative, then we begin to embody the paranormal superhuman ideal of leading a moral life as well as granting ourselves stewardship of the earth, with the concomitant skills and consciousness necessary to do so in a way that provides a generous and fulfilling life for every person, animal, and place on the globe.

Mark Reeder, January 1st 2024

* * *

Alan Megargle's Thoughts

Throughout my time investigating the paranormal and Bigfoot, I've never encountered a place quite like the Bradshaw Ranch. From the moment we arrived, I could tell there was something special about the ranch, something supernatural. The energy was strong, and there was an endless feeling of being watched. As our investigation unfolded, we began to make contact with various types of other-worldly beings in a way that seemed almost too easy. To me, they seemed to be guiding us, encouraging us to keep going, dig deeper, and try more things. This felt like a continuation of all my research but intensified all at once.

Each entity we encountered seemed to offer us a new piece of this puzzle. The technology we used helped us to interact and understand it in ways I could never have imagined. All of my encounters over the years have been deeply personal for me, and the Bradshaw Ranch activity was no different. These weren't simply chance encounters. These beings were present for our sake, for our benefit. Whether these were ghosts or spirits, alien entities, cryptids, or all of that combined, they appeared with a unified purpose. I believe that purpose is two-fold:

1. To help us open our minds to the universe, help us look beyond the world that we know, and unlock the mysteries within us. Show us the way to connect with our true selves, the self that lives on after our bodies die.
2. For our team, specifically, to share these ideas and lessons with the world through our films and books. I think they

are guiding us to help others in their pursuit of answers
and understanding of the true self.

In conclusion, the Bradshaw Ranch unlocked more of the mystery
for me and encouraged me to continue to pursue these answers. My
journey will continue, and my thoughts on this will evolve. I'm open
and ready for a new chapter to see what they show me next.

Alan Megargle January 1st, 2024

APPENDICES

APPENDIX A

BRADSHAW RANCH TRIANGLE

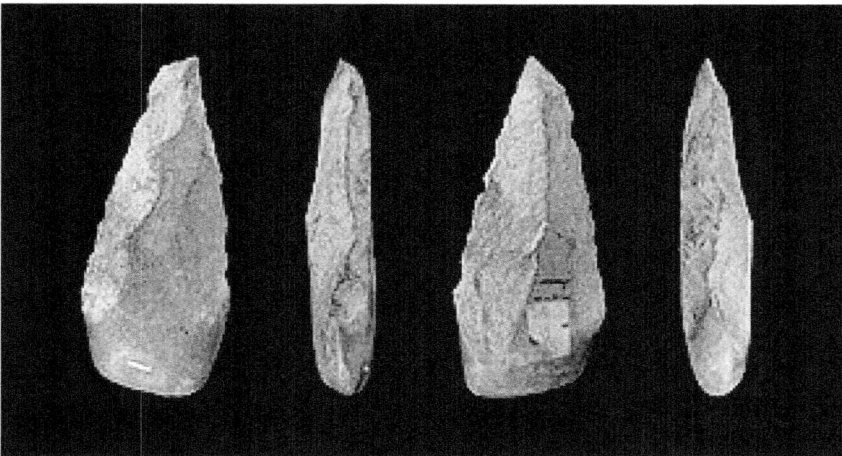

Figure 1: (Lower Paleolithic - Acheulan stone tools) photo by Didier Descouens from Museum de Toulouse

The triangle is one of the most dominant geometric shapes in nature. Many plants have triangular leaves or flowers, and some fruits, like cucumbers and melons, have a triangular center. Mountains are triangular, as are many rocks found on the ground.

Triangles are also prevalent throughout human history for their shape and beauty and their relationship to the occult and the paranormal. Our most ancient ancestors first employed the strength of the triangle shape in the flint spearheads they manufactured. Later, they created figurines of earth mothers in the shape of one triangle seated on the base of an inverted triangle. These earth mother gods assumed various names, such as Gaia and Isis. 4500 years ago, the ancient Egyptians and the Mayans recognized the triangle's strength as well as its occult meaning in the creation of the pyramids.

Interestingly, the triangle is featured in the Hebrew Ring of Solomon and in modern day Wiccan rites.

Triangles are prevalent in the occult and the paranormal because of the vortexes they can create. Vortexes that can lead mystic searchers to power, and fulfillment, and they can act as portals to other worlds. Examples of the power of these paranormal triangles around the world are the Nevada Triangle, the Great Lakes Triangle and the classic Bermuda Triangle in the Atlantic Ocean, and the Dragon Triangle in the Pacific Ocean, both of which are also known as the Devil's Triangles.

Figure 2:Earth Mother Goddess Catalhoyuk; photo by Nevit Dilmen Museum of Anatolian Civilizations 1320259

Figure 3: Pyramids of Giza; Wikimedia Commons; Photo by KennyOMG

Figure 4:Figure 3:Uxmal, Pyramid of the Magician; Wikimedia Commons; Photo by Runt35

Figure 5:Solomon's Ring, LapisLazuli; Wikimedia Commons; Photo by Pblpitt

Figure 6: Wiccan Pentacle; Museum of Witchcraft and Magic;
Photo by Ethan Doyle White

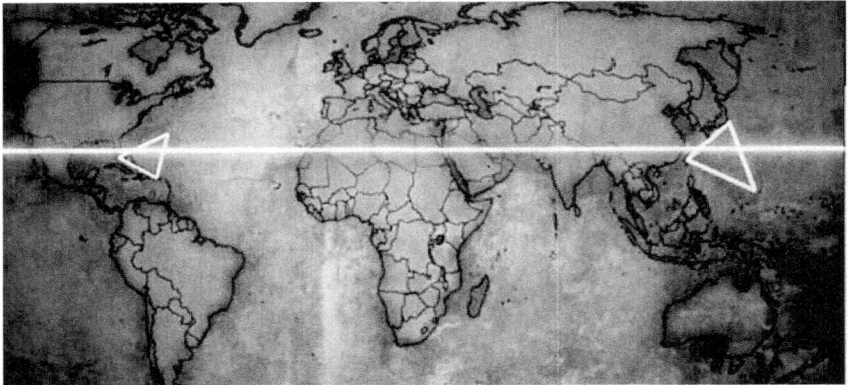

Figure 7:Map of the Bermuda and Dragon Triangles Locations; Wikimedia Commons;
photo by Parsa and Paper

APPENDIX B
ELECTROMAGNETIC FIELDS

Electromagnetic fields have existed for centuries, but their effect on humans has only been recorded and studied for decades. Scientists generally agree that low-frequency EMFs pose little danger to human health. But some researchers offer evidence that danger may exist over long-term use, specifically to the nervous system and the brain's cognitive functions. All devices connected to the electric power systems, including power lines, create extremely low-frequency EMFs, which are non-ionizing and generally harmless to humans. Higher frequency EMFs, such as x-rays and gamma rays, are ionizing, with the potential for cellular and DNA damage.

Radio

 AM radio

 Amateur radio

Microwave

 Aircraft communication

 Microwave oven

Infrared

 TV Remote Control

 Night vision goggles

Visible

Ultraviolet

 UV light from the Sun

X-ray

 Airport security scanner

Gamma-ray

PET scan

Terrestrial gamma-ray flashes

APPENDIX C
NATIVE AMERICANS, PORTALS, BRADSHAW RANCH, AND THE NEW PHYSICS

Bradshaw Ranch, our destination for investigating a paranormal hotspot similar to Skinwalker Ranch in Utah, lies in the heart of the Four Corners region of the Desert Southwest. This area is steeped in paranormal mystery and mystical activity dating back thousands of years. Visitors can see evidence of these phenomena in the Sedona, Arizona area and the valley's intriguing collection of Native American rock art ... at the remarkable cliff dwellings of the Anasazi in Mesa Verde, Colorado ... at the enchanted lands of Arizona's Canyon de Chelly National Monument ... and New Mexico's Petroglyph National Monument.

The stars, the moon, and the sun have long played a significant role in Native Americans' lives from the Atlantic to the Pacific. Aside from their practical use as navigation aids and temporal markers, they were viewed as conduits for ancestral spirits and otherworldly beings, usually referred to as Sky People or sometimes Star Beings and the now common 21st century expression, Star People.

One of the remarkable aspects common to Native American tribes in the Four Corners region is the shared belief that Star Beings from other worlds and dimensions have traveled to the Desert Southwest either through star ships or inter-dimensional portals. Indeed, many Native American cultures refer to Star Beings in their creation stories.

For example, the Iroquois creation story states that the earth was formed when Sky Woman fell from the sky into a large ocean and onto a giant turtle. Fish and birds brought her soil, which she used to form the earth on the turtle's back.

The First Nation Cree peoples of Canada believe that their ancestors arrived from the stars as spirits and then became human. The Hopi believe their ancestors came from the Pleiades, a cluster of stars in the constellation Taurus.

The Plains Indians have similar traditions. The Cheyenne have a name for the giant beings their ancestors ran into while migrating onto America's northern Great Plains. They called them *haztova hotoxceo* or "two-faced star people. Dakota legends tell of the Pleiades as the home of the ancestors. Tom Dongo's good friend, the Santee Shaman, Waykiniipicye, explained, "We came from the stars, Star People, Wicahpi-Oyate, and so back in our creation stories, we talk about how we came to earth and were placed here. There are several different types of Star People at different locations."

Also, among the Lakota, the holy man Black Elk told a story of his vision quest related in *Black Elk, The Sacred Ways of a Lakota* by Wallace Black Elk and William Lyon. "So when I went to vision quest, that disk came from above. The scientists call that a...Unidentified Flying Object, but that's a joke, see? Because they are not trained, they lost contact with the wisdom, power and gift....So that disk landed on top of me. It was concave, and there was another one on top of that. It was silent, but it lit and luminesced like neon lights. Even the sacred robes there were luminesced, and those tobacco ties lying there lit up like little light bulbs. Then these little people came, but each little group spoke a different language. They could read minds, and I could read their minds. I could read them. So there was silent communication. You could read it, like when you read silent symbols in a book. So we were able to communicate...They are human, so I welcomed them. I said, "Welcome, Welcome."

The oral traditions among the Desert Southwest Native Americans expressly tell of visits by Star Beings either through star ships or inter-dimensional portals. These Star People transmitted important information guiding agricultural practices and the delicate balance between nature and spirituality. As shown by the petroglyphs left behind by the Sinagua around Sedona thousands of years ago, the Star Beings arrived through portals and starships. Also, according to Frank Cushing, a 19th-century anthropologist, and ethnologist who documented New Mexico's Zuni Indians spiritual practices and beliefs, men and women were introduced to the earth through a series of caves and tunnels ending in a portal that led to the earth.

Figure 1: An Ancestral Puebloan Petroglyph in Mesa Verde National Park, Showing the Creation Story of the Ancestral Puebloans. Courtesy of the National Park Service

Star ships are commonly accepted in the 21st century as the means by which humankind will eventually visit the stars beyond our solar system. On the other hand, traveling from another dimension to our earth would appear impossible. Yet world history is replete with examples of such contacts. Many of these contacts take on a religious connotation.

Among nearly every culture in the world are myths of the origins of people by beings from the stars. The Greek and Egyptian panoplies of Gods and Goddesses are replete with Star Beings, who were the protectors and rulers of humankind. In Japanese mythology, Amaterasu was the goddess of the sun. Along with her siblings, the moon deity Tsukuyomi and the storm god Susanoo, she was considered one of the 'Three Precious Children' who brought life to the earth.

Figure 2: Amaterasu Emerging from a Cave and Shining Her Light on the Japanese Islands and People. Photo by Utagawa Kunisada

The Archangel Gabriel, the angel of revelation, acts as a messenger for God in Christianity, Islam, and Judaism. He often can be recognized as an amber light. Gabriel is perhaps best known for announcing the coming birth of Jesus to Mary and the shepherds.

In the Christian tradition, according to the Book of John in the New Testament, 20:19, three days after his crucifixion, Christ rose from the dead and appeared to the apostles: 'Then the same day at evening, being the first *day* of the week, when the doors were shut where the disciples were assembled for fear of the Jews, came Jesus and stood in the midst, and saith unto them, Peace *be* unto you."

In 312CE, the Roman Emperor Constantine was said to have seen an angel bearing a symbol of Jesus—Chi and Rho, the first two Greek letters of Christ's name—before he converted to Christianity and brought the entire Roman Empire with him.

Figure 3: Constantine's vision and the Battle of the Milvian Bridge in a 9th-century Byzantine manuscript from the Bibliothèque Nationale de France - Illustrated painted parchment Greek manuscript (879-883 AD)

Attila the Hun unexpectedly turned away from attacking Rome in 451CE when Pope Leo I, known as Leo the Great, met him outside the city. Pope Leo threatened the leader of the Huns with the power of St. Peter, the prince of the Apostles. For his own part, Attila was said to have been persuaded from sacking Rome in the heart of the Empire when visited by St. Peter.

Figure 4: The Meeting of Leo the Great and Attila, 1514, Stanza di Eliodoro, Raphael Rooms, Apostolic Palace, Vatican City

In a more secular setting, all of us have at least heard of, if not experienced, guardian angels who protect us from demons, ward off evil, strengthen our minds, and illuminate the truth. Famous country music star Dolly Parton tells the story of how her deceased grandmother warned her not to board a plane headed to Salt Lake City. Parton recalled, "I saw my grandma's ghost standing in the corner. She kept saying, 'Don't catch the plane... Don't catch the plane." Parton, heeding her grandmother's advice, switched flights. The flight she was supposed to be on crashed with no survivors.

In March 2015, Utah police officers investigating a partially submerged car in the Spanish Fork River, heard a young, female voice cry out from the car, "Help me, we're in here." Police pulled the wreck out of the river. Inside, they found Jennifer Groesbeck and her 18-month-old daughter, Lily. Jennifer had died hours before. Lily was barely conscious but alive. The disembodied voice helped them rescue the infant.

Where do these guardian angels and Native American Star Beings come from? We explored one concept in our first book, *The Bigfoot Alien Connection Revisited*. 20th-century physicist Albert Einstein's Theory of General Relativity mathematically predicted the existence of portals connecting distant points through space and time. Called Einstein-Rosen Bridges, these portals, also known as wormholes, are gateways to the past ... the future ... and other dimensions. On a cosmic scale, these unpredictable portals, sometimes known as black holes, cover vast interstellar distances. But what if they exist on the micro-scale, just large enough to allow beings to reach earth from another dimension?

Curiously, as we discovered on our second visit to Bradshaw Ranch, the evidence of the existence of portals to other dimensions lies in America's Desert Southwest, home to ancient Native American tribes who depicted stories about portals as well as visits by interdimensional beings in their rock art.

The events related in Native American stories are more than myths or wishful thinking, or legends. Each one of these encounters presupposes a non-human or super-human intelligence. They also imagine a paradigm shift in the means of travel between worlds as well as dimensions. Just as quantum mechanics provided an enhancement of Newtonian Physics, it is at Bradshaw Ranch that the culmination of the many historical paranormal encounters and present-day investigation into paranormal phenomena points to a new paradigm shift in our present-day understanding of the physics of interstellar travel ... communication ... and transmission of information.

AFTERWORD

Go to hangar1publishing.com to learn more about the Authors and stay up to date with their newest releases.

Printed in Dunstable, United Kingdom